COADJUTORS AND AUXILIARIES OF BISHOPS
A HISTORICAL SYNOPSIS AND A COMMENTARY

THE CATHOLIC UNIVERSITY OF AMERICA

CANON LAW STUDIES

No. 238

Coadjutors and Auxiliaries of Bishops

A Historical Synopsis and a Commentary

BY THE

REV. GEORGE EDWARD LYNCH, A.B., S.T.L., J.C.L.

PRIEST OF THE DIOCESE OF RALEIGH

A DISSERTATION

SUBMITTED TO THE FACULTY OF THE SCHOOL OF CANON LAW OF THE CATHOLIC UNIVERSITY OF AMERICA IN PARTIAL FULFILLMENT OF THE REQUIREMENTS FOR THE DEGREE OF DOCTOR OF CANON LAW

THE CATHOLIC UNIVERSITY OF AMERICA PRESS

WASHINGTON, D. C.

1947

NIHIL OBSTAT:

EDUARDUS G. ROELKER, S.T.D., J.C.D.

Censor Deputatus

Washington, D. C., die. XI iunii, 1946.

IMPRIMATUR:

✠ VINCENTIUS S. WATERS, D.D.

Episcopus Raleighiensis

Raleigh, die. XI iunii, 1946.

MURRAY & HEISTER
WASHINGTON, D. C.

PRINTED BY
TIMES AND NEWS PUBLISHING CO.
GETTYSBURG, PA., U. S. A.

TO

HIS EXCELLENCY
THE MOST REVEREND EUGENE J. McGUINNESS, D.D.

Former Bishop of Raleigh
and
Present Coadjutor of Tulsa-Oklahoma City

TABLE OF CONTENTS

TABLE OF CONTENTS (Continued)

PART II

CANONICAL COMMENTARY

FOREWORD

The purpose of this dissertation is twofold: first, to investigate the evidences of the office of assistant Bishops in the early centuries of Christianity, and to trace the gradual development of the various phases of that office through the centuries in so far as the available documents will permit; and secondly, to consider the legislation expressed in or related to canons 350 to 355 of the Code of Canon Law, which comprises the general subject, *De Coadiutoribus et Auxiliaribus Episcoporum.*

The present legislation of the Code concerning Coadjutor and Auxiliary Bishops has always had its counterpart in Church legislation since the second or third century. Although the terms used to designate the office were not always uniform, the basic notion was always present. For wherever Christianity became strong in the number of its adherents it was natural that the ruling Bishop needed assistance to care properly for his diocese, both in matters relating to the power of orders and in matters involving the power of jurisdiction. It was therefore to be expected that an office similar to the present institution of Coadjutor Bishops should be introduced at an early stage in the history of Christianity. Moreover, in the appointment of Coadjutor Bishops the Church has shown at once her desire to provide in a fitting manner for the welfare of the faithful, and her unwillingness to deprive of his see any disabled Bishop who has faithfully fulfilled his duties.

The office of the Coadjutor Bishop is no less important today than it has been in past centuries. With the gradual increase in the numbers of the faithful this office may be expected to assume even a greater importance. In any diocese or archdiocese with a predominantly Catholic population the appointment of a Coadjutor Bishop to share the burdens of the Ordinary in the exercise of episcopal orders or jurisdiction becomes imperative. Or again, when the residential Bishop of a diocese becomes disabled, it is necessary for the Church to continue its past policy of assigning a Coadjutor to perform his duties while the former retains his office as principal Bishop of the diocese.

In addition to a commentary on canons 350 to 355, consideration has been given in the following pages to various canonical problems connected with the office of Coadjutorship. Most commentaries written since the promulgation of the Code give only a brief treatment of the canons on Coadjutors and Auxiliaries of Bishops. Consequently they either omit or only briefly refer to these problems. Since these problems are nevertheless of practical import, a careful consideration of them together with an attempt at a possible solution is fully justified.

The writer wishes to express his gratitude to their Excellencies, the Most Rev. Vincent S. Waters, Bishop of Raleigh, and the Most Rev. Eugene J. McGuinness, former Bishop of Raleigh and present Coadjutor Bishop of Tulsa-Oklahoma City, for the opportunity of advanced study at the Catholic University of America. He is also grateful to the members of the Faculty of the School of Canon Law at the Catholic University for their kind assistance in the preparation of this study.

PART I

HISTORICAL SYNOPSIS

Of the three chapters comprising this part of the dissertation, the first will be concerned with the existence of Coadjutor Bishops in various parts of the Christian world previous to the time of Gratian, when legislation on the subject was neither consistent nor universal, as a result mainly of the difficulties of intercommunication. In the second chapter, which will consider the more universal legislation from the time of Gratian to the Council of Trent, it will be possible to choose logical divisions according to the various phases of the office, and within these divisions to treat each phase chronologically. The third chapter, treating of the post-Tridentine legislation on the subject, will necessarily be brief. There was no radical change in the office after the Council of Trent, and there was little additional legislation other than the particular application of principles in decisions rendered by the Roman Congregations.

CHAPTER I

Pre-Gratian Legislation

An institution of ancient times very similar to the present ecclesiastical office of the Auxiliary and Coadjutor Bishop was that of the *Chorepiscopi* or 'Rural Bishops' (Χωρεπίσκοποι). There were some *Chorepiscopi* in the Eastern Church probably as early as the middle of the second century. This institution was later introduced into the Western Church, where the *Chorepiscopi* gradually assumed many of the duties and prerogatives at present associated with Auxiliary and Coadjutor Bishops.

In the first centuries of the propagation of Christianity the work of conversion was confined almost exclusively to the large towns and cities of the Roman Empire. It was only after Christianity had become firmly established in the more populous communities that the ministers of the Gospel turned their attention to the more sparsely populated sections of the surrounding countryside. In aid of the Bishop for the administration of the rural districts of the diocese the office of *Chorepiscopus* was established. *Chorepiscopi* were appointed for these rural districts which continued subject to the Bishop in the city. The history of the *Chorepiscopi* may usefully be summarized here, since they had at least this in common with the present day Auxiliary and Coadjutor Bishops, that the incumbent had some episcopal powers and assisted the Bishop in the rule of the diocese.

It is hardly necessary for the purpose of this dissertation to discuss whether all these *Chorepiscopi* were Bishops, whether only some of them were, or whether all of them were merely priests with some of the powers of the Bishop granted to them. The question has long been disputed, and a conclusive proof seems impossible. Thomassinus (1619-1695)[1] and Pope Benedict XIV (1740-1758)[2] maintained that at least some of the *Chorepiscopi*

[1] *Vetus et Nova Ecclesiae Disciplina circa Beneficia et Beneficiarios* (10 vols. in 5, Magontiaci, 1787), Pars I, Lib. II, caput 1.

[2] Benedictus XIV, *De Synodo Dioecesana* (2 vols., Romae, 1806), Lib. III, cap. 3, n. 6.

had episcopal powers. Hinschius (1835-1898)[3] in his discussion of this point mentions, among others, the theory that they were only priests who held a rank superior to that of the other priests in their respective rural districts. This latter theory is generally rejected at the present time.

ARTICLE 1. *Chorepiscopi* IN THE EAST

The earliest available text mentioning the *Chorepiscopi* is that which Eusebius of Caesarea (ca. 263-339) incorporated in his *Ecclesiastical History,* a letter issued against Paul of Samosata by the Council of Antioch (269), which distinguishes between Bishops of the city and of the country districts.[4] The prevalence of this institution of the *Chorepiscopi* in the fourth century in the East is evident from the legislation of the Eastern Councils of that period. The Provincial Council of Neocaesarea in Pontus (314-325), in a canon often cited by later councils, refers to *Chorepiscopi* as typified by or as patterned after the seventy disciples of Our Lord who assisted the Apostles, and thus indicates their subservience to the Bishops who are the successors of the Apostles.[5]

The thirteenth canon of the Provincial Council of Ancyra in Phrygia (314) ruled that it was unlawful for these *Chorepiscopi* to ordain priests or deacons without the permission of the Bishop. This canon seems to imply that the *Chorepiscopi* could confer minor orders when necessary, even without consulting the Bishop.[6]

---

[3] P. Hinschius, *System des katholischen Kirchenrechts* (4 vols., Berlin, 1869-1888), II, 162.

[4] Eusebius, *Historia Ecclesiastica,* lib. VII, cap. 30, n. 10; ". . . επισκόπους τῶν ὁμορων ἀγρῶν τε καὶ πολέων."—Migne, *Patrologiae Cursus Completus, Series Graeca* (161 vols., Parisiis, 1856-1866), XX, 714. Hereinafter this will be cited *MPG.*

[5] Can. 14—Mansi, *Sacrorum Conciliorum Nova et Amplissima Collectio* (53 vols. in 60, Parisiis, 1901-1927) II, 541. Hereinafter this work will be cited as Mansi.

[6] "Chorepiscopos non licere presbyteros vel diaconos ordinare, sed neque urbis presbyteros, nisi cum literis ab episcopo permissum fuerit, in aliena paroechia."—Mansi, II, 518.

The *Chorepiscopi* were mentioned by the Ecumenical Council of Nicaea (325) when it considered the problem of receiving into the Church those who were members of the clergy among the Novatians. After a written profession of faith, they were to be received into the Church with the same clerical rank which they had as Novatians. However, those who were Bishops among the Novatians were not to have the rule of a diocese, but only the rank of priest (*presbyter*), unless the Bishop of the diocese saw fit to confer on them the rank of *Chorepiscopus.*[7]

The Provincial Council of Antioch in Syria (341) defined certain limits, similar to those set by the Council of Ancyra, beyond which the *Chorepiscopi* could not act. They were forbidden to interfere in the administration of churches other than those given to their charge, "even though they had received ordination to the Episcopate." Further, they were permitted to ordain lectors, exorcists, and subdeacons, but not deacons or priests unless the bishop of the city consented.[8]

Some councils tried to discourage the practice of ordaining these *Chorepiscopi,* probably because of the danger that these men might assume too much power (or had already done so) and come into conflict with the Bishops to whom they should be subject. The Council of Sardica in Dacia (343) forbade the ordination of a Bishop in places where one priest was sufficient, and preferred that new sees be established in places where the number of the faithful was large.[9] The Council of Laodicaea in Phrygia (343-381) ruled that priests should be appointed as visitors in the country districts (subject in all things to the Bishop of the city) to replace the rural Bishops.[10]

But despite these rulings of the councils, the institution of the *Chorepiscopi* did not yet die out in the East. In the fifth century the Ecumenical Council of Chalcedon (451), taking for granted the office of *Chorepiscopus,* did not legislate against it, but only

---

[7] Can. 8—Mansi, II, 671.

[8] Can. 10—Mansi, II, 1311.

[9] Can. 6—Mansi III, 10.

[10] Can. 57—*Canones Apostolorum et Conciliorum Saec. IV-VII* (ed. Bruns, 2 vols., Berolini: apud G. Geimeri, 1839), I, 79. Hereinafter this will be cited Bruns.

warned against simony in its conferral.[11] The VII Ecumenical Council, the II of Nicaea (787) mentioned briefly that according to the ancient custom *Chorepiscopi* could appoint lectors with the permission of the city Bishop.[12]

After the eighth century the office of the *Chorepiscopi* declined in the East and is seldom mentioned in later documents (though there are still chorbishops in several Oriental rites). Strangely enough, this decline came at the very time that the office began to assume importance in the Western Church.

ARTICLE 2. *Chorepiscopi* IN THE WEST

It was natural that the institution of the *Chorepiscopi* which began in the East should later be adopted by the Western Church, and there are many examples in the West of clerics with limited episcopal powers, although the term *Chorepiscopus* is not always applied to them.

One of the most noted examples of the appointment of an assistant Bishop in the early centuries of the Church is that of St. Augustine who, at the request of Bishop Valerius of Hippo, was made co-Bishop of that see. At the time both Valerius and Augustine were unaware that the eighth canon of the I Ecumenical Council of Nicaea (325) had forbidden the simultaneous rule of a diocese by two Bishops.[13]

In the year 439 the Council of Riez (*Regensis*) deposed a certain Bishop Armentarius who, contrary to a ruling of the Metropolitan Hilary of Arles (✠ 449), had been consecrated by two Bishops, neither of whom was a Metropolitan. However, he was granted certain episcopal rights, such as the administration of the Sacrament of Confirmation, but not that of ordaining even minor clerics. Thus, although the term *Chorepiscopus* is used, Bishop Armentarius had even less power than the Eastern *Chorepiscopus*.[14]

---

[11] Can. 2—Mansi, VII, 373.

[12] Can. 14—Mansi XIII, 753.

[13] Migne, *Patrologise Cursus Completus, Series Latina* (221 vols., Parisiis, 1844-1864), XXXIII, 967. Hereinafter this will be cited *MPL*.

[14] Mansi, V, 1192 ff.

St. Gregory of Tours (538-594) in his *History of the Franks* mentioned a Bishop who had the right of succession to a see similarly as the Coadjutor Bishop of today. He reported that a convert to the Church, named Austrapius, was by order of King Clotaire I (✠ 561) consecrated as Bishop of Poitiers (*circa* 556) with right of succession upon the death of Bishop Pientius (✠ after 561), who then ruled that see. Actually he never ruled the see because he did not enjoy the favor of King Charibert (✠ 567), who succeeded Clotaire I.[15] It is certain that he was the equivalent of a *Chorepiscopus,* for he was to govern a number of parishes in the village of Celles-sur-Belles.[16]

St. Gregory also recorded another instance of a Coadjutor Bishop with the right of succession. In the diocese of Langres about the year 562 a certain Modericus was consecrated and assigned the task of directing the diocese until the death of Bishop Tetricus (✠ 573), when he was to succeed him. As in the case of Austrapius, Modericus never ruled the see, since he had lost the king's favor.[17] This is another example of a *Chorepiscopus,* for he was given charge of Tonnerre in Burgundy as archpriest.[18]

The appointment of Bishops as assistants to other Bishops became more frequent in the seventh and eighth centuries, especially in the missionary areas of Europe where the dioceses were so vast that one Bishop could not properly administer his diocese alone. Thus, as St. Boniface (✠ 754) related in a letter to Pope Stephen III (752-757), Bishop Willibrord of Frisia (✠ 739), when overtaken by old age, had appointed a *"corepiscopus"* to perform his duties.[19] For the same reason, Boniface had a *Chore-*

---

[15] Gregory of Tours, *Historia Francorum,* Liber IV, c. 18—*MPL,* LXXI, 284.

[16] Gottlob, *Der abendländische Chorepiskopat* (Bonn: Kurt Schroeder Verlag, 1928), p. 11. Hereinafter this work will be cited *Chorepiskopat.*

[17] *Historia Francorum,* Liber V, c. 5—*MPL,* LXXI, 321.

[18] Gottlob, *Chorepiskopat,* p. 12.

[19] *Monumenta Germaniae Historica, Epistolae Selectae,* Tomus I, *Bonifatii et Lulli Epistolae* (ed. Michael Tangl, Berolini: apud Weidmannos, 1916), p. 235. Hereinafter this will be cited as *MGH, Ep. sel.*

piscopus named Eobanus (✠ 754) to whom he had given the bishopric of Utrecht.[20]

That the office of *Chorepiscopus* was a common one at this time may be seen from other ninth century documents, which mention *Chorepiscopi* without discussing them in detail. Thus, three *Chorepiscopi* are listed as present at a Council in Mainz in 829,[21] and four attended another Council in the same city in 852.[22]

During these centuries *Chorepiscopi* are also to be found in the Frankish Kingdom as well as in the missionary dioceses of Germany.

In the year 747 Pepin (✠ 768) inquired of Pope Zacharias (741-752) regarding the honor due to Metropolitans by the *Chorepiscopi.* In replying to this question the Pope quoted the tenth canon of the Council of Antioch (341).[23] Another letter[24] was written by the same Pope in 748 to "the Bishops and the beloved *Chorepiscopi*" from which Gottlob[25] conjectures that the *Chorepiscopi* at that time were either missionary Bishops or the Coadjutors of Bishops.

In this same year (748) an important reply was sent by Pope Zacharias to St. Boniface, Bishop of Mainz. So important was it that it was included in the *Decretum* of Gratian.[26] St. Boniface,

[20] *Monumenta Germaniae Historica, Scriptores Rerum Germanarum, Vita Sancti Bonifatii auctore Willibaldo* (recognovit Wilhelmus Levison, Hannoverae et Lipsiae, 1905), p. 47, lines 20 ff. Hereinafter this will be cited as *MGH, Script. Rer. Germ.*

[21] *Monumenta Germaniae Historica, Legum Sectio III, Concilia, Aevi Merowingici,* Tomus II, Pars 2 (ed. Albertus Werminghoff, Hannoverae et Lipsiae, 1908), p. 604. Hereinafter this will be cited as *MGH, Concilia.*

[22] *Monumenta Germaniae Historica, Legum Sectio II, Capitularia Regum Francorum,* Tomus II, Pars Prior (edd. Alfredus Boretius et Victor Krause, Hannoverae, 1890), p. 185. Hereinafter this will be cited as *MGH, Capitularia.*

[23] *MGH, Epistolae,* Tomus III, *Merowingici et Karolini Aevi I* (ed. Ericus Caspar, Berolini: apud Weidmannos, 1925), p. 480. Hereinafter this will be cited as *MGH, Epistolae.*

[24] *MGH, Ep. sel.,* I, 182.

[25] *Chorepiskopat,* p. 102.

[26] C. 17, C. VII, q. 1: Jaffé, Philippus, *Regesta Pontificum Romanorum ab condita Ecclesia ad annum post Christum natum MCXCVIII* (ed. 2, 2 vols. in 1, Lipsiae: 1885-1888), n. 2264. Hereinafter this will be cited as Jaffé.

because of his old age, requested of the Pope a Coadjutor who would succeed him as Bishop of Mainz. The request for a Coadjutor was granted, and by special privilege Boniface was allowed to choose a worthy successor, but only at the hour of his death and before witnesses.[27] The Coadjutor chosen by St. Boniface about the year 752 was Lullus (✠ 786), a subject of the Abbot Fulcred (✠ 784), from whom permission was received that he be made a *Chorepiscopus*.[28]

The subordination of the *Chorepiscopus* to the Bishop of the diocese is evident in a letter sent in 798 by the Metropolitan Arno of Salzburg (785-821) to his suffragan Bishops, in which he invited them to a Council, and told them to command their *Chorepiscopi* to be present.[29]

A capitulary issued in 789 warned the *Chorepiscopi* to do nothing without the permission of the Bishop of the district. Thus it is seen that the same tendency to extend their authority unlawfully, which has already been noted among the *Chorepiscopi* of the East, was true also in the Western Church.[30] The *Chorepiscopi* were assuming more and more power, and accordingly a reaction against this aggrandizement was inevitable. Hincmar, Archbishop of Rheims (845-882), in a letter to Pope Leo IV (847-855) in 851 revealed that *Chorepiscopi* often ruled dioceses during the vacancy of the see.[31]

The reaction against this usurpation of power by the *Chorepiscopi* did not begin in earnest until the Council of Paris in 829. To point out the subordinate character of the *Chorepiscopi* in relation to Bishops, the Council repeated the fourteenth canon of the Council on Neocesarea (314-325), which compared *Chorepiscopi* to the 70 disciples, while it considered the Bishops as the successors of the Apostles. The *Chorepiscopi* were forbidden to confer the sacrament of Confirmation, and were warned not to act beyond the powers granted by the Councils. Moreover, Bishops

---

[27] *MGH, Ep. sel.*, I, 180.

[28] *MGH, Ep. sel.*, I, 213; cf. also Gottlob, *Chorepiskopat*, p. 23.

[29] *MGH, Concilia*, II, 196.

[30] *MGH, Capitularia*, I, 54.

[31] Flodoardus, *Historia Remensis Ecclesiae*, Lib. III, caput 10—*MGH, Scriptores*, XIII (ed. G. Waitz, Hannoverae, 1881), 482-483.

were forbidden to transfer more power to them than that which was indicated for them in the traditional canons.[32]

During this reaction against the *Chorepiscopi,* Rhabanus Maurus (*circa* 780-856), Abbot of Fulda (822-842) and later Archbishop of Mainz (847-856), defended them, giving an affirmative answer to the question: "Si liceat chorepiscopis presbyteros et diaconos ordinare cum consensu episcopi sui?"[33] He also claimed that one of the main reasons for their institution by the Church was to administer Confirmation in the country districts.[34] But despite this defense the movement to suppress the *Chorepiscopi* gradually gathered strength.

An appendix to Flodoard's *History of the Church of Rheims* contains a ruling made about the year 840 by Ebo, Archbishop of that city (816-845), in which he enumerated the duties of a *Chorepiscopus.* According to Ebo the work of the *Chorepiscopus* was almost identical with that of other priests, except for certain consecrations which were to be performed only by order of the Bishop.[35]

In 845 the Council of Meaux forbade *Chorepiscopi* to consecrate churches or to confirm. It permitted them to confer Holy Orders only with the Bishop's permission, and even then not beyond the subdiaconate. They were furthermore forbidden to rule any diocese during the vacancy of the see, since this practice often caused too great a delay in the appointment of a new Bishop. The Council prescribed the deposition of the *Chorepiscopus* for any violation of these rules.[36]

The decline of the *Chorepiscopi* in the Western Church was further accelerated during this period by the appearance of the Pseudo-Isidorian forgeries. Among the reforms attempted through these spurious documents was the lessening of the power of the *Chorepiscopi.*

Taking the seventh canon of the II Council of Seville (618),[37]

---

[32] *MGH, Concilia,* II, 629 ff.

[33] *MPL,* CX, 1195 ff.

[34] *MPL,* CVII, 301.

[35] *MPL,* CXXXV, 409 ff.

[36] *MGH, Capitularia,* II, 409 ff.

[37] Mansi, X, 559.

which condemned the practice of allowing priests to perform functions reserved to Bishops, the forgers added the term *Chorepiscopi.* The result was that the prohibitions seemed to apply to *Chorepiscopi* as well as to priests. The document was then represented as a letter of Pope Leo the Great (440-461) to the Bishops of Germany and Gaul.[38] By it *Chorepiscopi* were forbidden to ordain priests and deacons, to consecrate virgins, to bless or consecrate altars, to confirm, and to reconcile sinners. This spurious document was later included by Gratian in his *Decretum.*[39]

A decree which the Pseudo-Isidorian forgers attributed to Pope Damasus (366-384) contains almost the identical prohibition as that attributed to Pope Leo the Great. One portion of this letter, which Gratian[40] also included, declares that the institution of the *Chorepiscopi* is condemned by the Holy See and by all Bishops.[41]

Finally, a decree falsely assigned to Pope John III (561-574) pretends to cite as genuine the foregoing forgeries assigned to Popes Leo and Damasus, and proceeds to demand the complete suppression of the *Chorepiscopi.*[42]

Since these Pseudo-Isidorian decretals were universally accepted in good faith as genuine, it is hardly surprising that the institution of the *Chorepiscopi* had all but disappeared by the time of Gratian, whose *Decretum* mentions them only to condemn them.[43]

About the year 865 Pope Nicholas I (858-867), in replying to Archbishop Rodolphus of Bourges (840-866), stated that ordinations of priests and deacons performed by *Chorepiscopi* who had been deposed by their Bishops were certainly unlawful, but were to be considered valid.[44]

In the present chapter there have been cited many examples of clerics who in the early Middle Ages performed the functions

---

38 Hinschius, *Decretales Pseudo-Isidorianae et Capitula Angilramni* (Lipsiae, 1863), p. 628. Hereinafter this will be cited as Hinschius.

39 C. 4, D. 68.

40 C. 5, D. 68.

41 Hinschius, pp. 510-513.

42 Hinschius, p. 715.

43 C. 5, D. 68.

44 *MGH, Epistolae Karolini, Aevi IV, Tomus VI* (ed. Ernestus Perels, Berolini apud Weidmannos, 1925), 634.

of Coadjutors of Bishops. Sometimes they were referred to as *Chorepiscopi,* sometimes as Bishops. These examples are sufficient to show that the institution of assistant Bishops was a common one previous to the time of Gratian, though naturally it was not as clearly defined or canonically established as it became in later centuries.

After the eleventh century the power formerly associated with the *Chorepiscopi* became extinct. However, the title *Chorepiscopus* remained and was applied in the Western Church to such persons of non-episcopal character as the archdeacon, the provost, or the dean of the Cathedral Chapter.[45] In what follows, the Coadjutor Bishops will be considered as an institution distinct from the *Chorepiscopi.*

---

[45] Cf. Gottlob, *Chorepiskopat,* pp. 141 ff.

CHAPTER II

Post-Gratian Legislation to the Council of Trent

With the appearance of Gratian's *Decretum* (*circa* 1140) and the subsequent Decretals of Pope Gregory IX (1234) and the *Liber Sextus* of Pope Boniface VIII (1298), the legislation concerning Coadjutor Bishops becomes clearer, more explicit, and more detailed. In each of these collections are gathered previously existing and newly formed decrees which served as a basis for the legislation on this institution in later centuries.

Gratian's *Decretum* records several examples of the appointment of Coadjutors for disabled Bishops. One is a reply of Pope Gregory I (590-604) to the Deacon Anatolius at Constantinople, who had asked him to appoint another Bishop to replace the ailing Bishop at Skoplye (*prima Justiniana*). The Pope refused this request, saying that it would be unjust and contrary to the traditional procedure. He permitted instead that a Coadjutor be chosen for the benefit of both Bishop and people.[1] Similar replies were given by Pope Gregory I to Bishop Eleutherius[2] and by Pope Nicholas I (858-867) to Aliunus, Archbishop of Genoa,[3] who had asked whether illness justified the removal of a Bishop. The permission given by Pope Zachary (741-752) to St. Boniface to choose a Coadjutor has been noted in the previous chapter.[4]

During the reign of Pope Gregory I, the Bishop of Rimini had travelled to Rome and asked permission of the Pope to be relieved of his office because of illness. He was persuaded to retain his office because of a possible recovery. After four years the clergy of the diocese appealed to the Pope, who replied that a Coadjutor should be elected and sent to Rome with the decree of election.[5]

[1] C. 1, C. VII, q. 1; Jaffé, n. 1819.
[2] C. 14, C. VII, q. 1; Jaffé, n. 1872.
[3] C. 4, C. VII, q. 1; Jaffé, n. 2846.
[4] C. 17, C. VII, q. 1; Jaffé, n. 2264.
[5] C. 13, C. VII, q. 1; Jaffé, n. 1663.

In the year 1204 Pope Innocent III (1198-1216) received a petition for the appointment of a Coadjutor for the Bishop of Orange, who was suffering from an incurable disease. The people of that diocese had previously petitioned the Metropolitan Archbishop of Arles, who in turn referred the matter to the Pope. The Pope ordered the Metropolitan to choose a suitable candidate as Coadjutor.[6]

Finally, mention should be made of an important document issued by Pope Boniface VIII (1294-1303), in which he reserved to the Holy See the granting of Coadjutors of Bishops.[7]

These few examples of the appointment of Coadjutor Bishops indicate how this office had developed during the several centuries previous to Gratian and shortly thereafter. The legislation which accompanied these appointments will be the subject of the following pages.

ARTICLE I. NOTION AND PURPOSE OF THE COADJUTOR BISHOP

Although the appointment of someone to assist a Bishop who is unable to fulfill the duties of his office must be admitted as a dictate of reason, medieval commentators, such as Ioannes Andreae (1272-1348)[8] and Panormitanus (1386-1453),[9] pointed to the *Digest* of Justinian[10] for its counterpart in Roman Law. They said that just as the term *tutor* is derived from the verb *tueor* (to care for), so the canonical term *Coadjutor* is derived from *coadiuvare* (to assist).

The purpose of granting a Coadjutor Bishop was twofold: the welfare of the Bishop to whom he was given, and the care

---

[6] C. 5, X, *de clerico aegrotante vel debilitato,* III, 6; Potthast, Augustus, *Regesta Pontificum Romanorum inde ab anno post Christum natum MCXCVIII ad annum MCCCIV* (2 vols., Berolini, 1874-1875), n. 2335. Hereinafter this will be cited as Potthast.

[7] C. un., *de clerico aegrotante vel debilitato,* III, 5, in VI°.

[8] *Commentaria in Quinque Decretalium Libros Novella* (Venetiis, 1581), Lib. III, tit. 6, c. 6, n. 4. Hereafter this will be cited *Novella.*

[9] *Commentaria in Quinque Decretalium Libros* (5 vols. in 7, Venetiis, 1588), Lib. III, tit. 6, c. 6, n. 1. Hereinafter this will be cited *Commentaria.*

[10] D. (26, 1), 1.

of the souls entrusted to that Bishop. Thus the letter of Pope Innocent III to the Archbishop of Arles,[11] stated: "Therefore, wishing to provide in a salutary manner both for the aforementioned Bishop and for his Church, . . . we command that you assign him as Coadjutor a prudent and worthy man through whom care may be had for the Bishop and for the people entrusted to him." The same notion is indicated by Gratian's text taken from the letter of Pope Gregory I to Anatolius at Constantinople.[12]

It was always the policy of the Holy See to insist that a Bishop who was inculpably hindered from performing his pastoral duties should not be removed from office, but rather given someone to assist him. Pope Innocent III cited the principle: *"Afflictis non est addenda afflictio."*[13] Pope Gregory I claimed that it had never been customary to appoint another Bishop to a see on account of the illness of the incumbent, because it would be unjust that an ailing incumbent should be deprived of his office.[14]

Medieval commentators discussed the question whether or not a Coadjutor Bishop was to be considered a Prelate. The Gloss on the words *Curam animarum* affirmed that he was a Prelate for the reason that he had the care of souls.[15] Later commentators on this text, however, generally disagreed with the Gloss, and maintained that a Coadjutor Bishop was not, strictly considered, a Prelate. They distinguished between a *prelatus quoad ius* and a *prelatus quoad exercitium.* Since the ailing Bishop no longer exercised his office he could not be a *prelatus quoad exercitium,* but nonetheless he remained a *prelatus quoad ius.* The Coadjutor was never a *prelatus quoad ius,* and only in the sense that he had the exercise of the office could he be referred to as a *prelatus quoad exercitium.* Panormitanus stated that a Prelate was meant to have the free administration of all income, and that since the

---

[11] C. 5, X, *de clerico aegrotante vel debilitato,* III, 6.

[12] C. 1, C. VII, q. 1.

[13] C. 5, X, *de clerico aegrotante vel debilitato,* III, 6.

[14] C. 1, C. VII, q. 1; cf. also the *Glossa Ordinaria* ad c. un., *de clerico aegrotante vel debilitato,* III, 5 in VI°, s. v. *perpetuo.*

[15] C. 3, X, *de clerico aegrotante vel debilitato,* III, 6.

Coadjutor controlled only a portion of it, he could not be considered as a Prelate.[16]

At times a Coadjutor was granted to a Bishop to administer only the temporal matters in a diocese. At other times he was appointed to provide only for the spiritual care of souls.[17] Usually however, his office included duties in both temporal and spiritual matters. The legislation in the *Corpus Iuris Canonici* does not make this distinction, but it was implied by later commentators.[18]

ARTICLE 2. QUALIFICATIONS OF THE COADJUTOR BISHOP

The qualities required of a Coadjutor Bishop were in general those which were demanded of a Bishop or anyone entrusted with high office in the Church. The previously mentioned letter of Pope Gregory I stated that the candidate should be one who enjoys a good reputation, and moreover one who "can be worthy of the rule of a church, and think of the welfare of souls, restrain the unruly under the bond of discipline, take care of ecclesiastical matters, and show himself mature and effective in all things. . . ." The Pope then added that the specified candidate should be consecrated as a Bishop.[19]

These ideas were similarly expressed by Pope Zachary (741-752)[20] and Pope Innocent III (1198-1216).[21] Ioannes Andreae[22] and Panormitanus[23] distinguished between the Coadjutor given

[16] *Commentaria,* Lib. III, tit. 6, c. 3, n. 6; cf. Hostiensis [Henricus de Segusio], *In Quinque Decretalium Libros Commentaria* (5 vols. in 3, Venetiis, 1581), Lib. III, tit. 6, c. 3: ". . . tamquam coadiutor, et quo ad exercitium, et praelatus nihilominus quo ad ius remanet, sed non quo ad exercitium . . ."; cf. Ioannes Andreae, *Novella,* Lib. III, tit. 6, c. 3, n. 1. Cf. also Boich, Henricus, *In Quinque Decretalium Libros Commentaria* (Venetiis, 1576), Lib. III, tit. 6, c. 6, n. 8. Hereinafter this will be cited as Boich.

[17] Ioannes Andreae, *Novella,* Lib. III, tit. 6, c. 6, n. 9.

[18] "Officium est habere curam ecclesiae, et spiritualium et temporalium."—Ioannes Andreae, *Novella,* Lib. III, tit. 6, c. 5, n. 8.

[19] C. 14, C. VII, q. 1.

[20] C. 17, C. VII, q. 1; Jaffé, n. 2264.

[21] C. 5, X, *de clerico aegrotante vel debilitato,* III, 6.

[22] *Novella,* Lib. III, tit. 5, c. un.

[23] *Commentarium,* Lib. III, tit. 5, c. un.

for temporal affairs only and the one given for the care of souls without the care of temporal affairs. They stated that the capabilities of the one chosen should be considered with a view to the character of the work to which he was to be appointed.

Regarding the minimum age of a Coadjutor Bishop, Ioannes Andreae taught that a man of twenty-five years could be assigned to that office.[24] Panormitanus,[25] on the contrary, held that for a Coadjutor who was given to a Bishop it was necessary that he have completed his thirtieth year, since that was the minimum age requirement for all Bishops. He took cognizance of the opinion of Ioannes Andreae, and conceded that, if the Coadjutor was granted only for temporal matters, then twenty-five years of age sufficed (for at this age Roman Law permitted one to be a *tutor, curator,* or *procurator*). But he added that, if the office included the care of souls, then the Coadjutor had to be thirty years of age.

As to the question whether a religious could be given to a Bishop as a Coadjutor, Ioannes Andreae[26] and Panormitanus[27] agreed that it was lawful to do so. At first Ioannes Andreae stated that ordinarily the work of a religious is only for the benefit of his monastery,[28] but later he qualified this by saying that he can be made a Coadjutor if the work is compatible with his state of life, and if he also has the permission of his religious superior.[29] Ioannes Andreae contemplated only the instance of a Coadjutor whose task was temporary, and therefore not invested with the right of future succession.

Panormitanus cited Ioannes Andreae in support of his argument, and dismissed the objection of the possible conflict with the religious state of life by saying that, if the common good of

---

[24] *Novella,* Lib. III, tit. 6, c. 6, n. 5: ". . . sufficiet quod attigerit 25 annum. Quod verum puto. In episcopatu requiritur quod perfecerit 30, de hoc dubito."

[25] *Op. cit.,* Lib. III, tit. 5, c. un.

[26] *Novella,* Lib. III, tit. 6, c. 6, n. 5.

[27] *Op. cit.,* Lib. III, tit. 6, c. 6.

[28] ". . . an religiosus dari possit coadiutor? Videtur quod non: quia non potest procurare, vel postulare nisi pro utilitate monasterii sui . . ."—Novella, *loc. cit.*

[29] "Credo religiosum dari posse coadiutorem illis officiis quibus posset praefici. . . ."

the Church so demanded, then this necessity superseded the claims of the contemplative way of life.[30]

The Council of Trent in treating of Coadjutor Bishops decreed that the same qualifications which the law required in all Bishops were also required of those given as Coadjutors.[31]

ARTICLE 3. BY WHOM A COADJUTOR WAS GRANTED

Pope Gregory I, in writing to the Deacon Anatolius at Constantinople,[32] and later to Bishop Eleutherius,[33] allowed the appointment of a Coadjutor Bishop by the proper authorities in the diocese itself when the circumstances made this action advisable. In the latter case he mentioned that an election was to be held. Again, Pope Zachary in 748 allowed St. Boniface, Archbishop of Mainz, to choose a suitable Coadjutor,[34] and Pope Innocent III in 1204 commanded the Metropolitan Archbishop of Arles to provide a Coadjutor Bishop for the Diocese of Orange.[35]

Pope Boniface VIII (1294-1303) was the first Roman Pontiff to declare expressly that the granting of Coadjutors for Bishops was to be included among the so called *causae maiores,* and therefore was reserved to the Holy See.[36] No custom contrary to this law was to be admitted in the future, nor was any prescription, however long, possible against the Holy See in matters which it thus reserved to itself.[37]

Ioannes Andreae in the Gloss for this text recalled the aforementioned letters of Pope Innocent III to the Archbishop of Arles and of Pope Gregory I to Anatolius at Constantinople.

---

[30] *Op. cit.,* Lib. III, tit. 6, c. 6, n. 4.

[31] Conc. Trident., sess. XXV, *de ref.* c. 7.

[32] C. 1, C. VII, q. 1; Jaffé, n. 1819.

[33] C. 14, C. VII, q. 1; Jaffé, n. 1872.

[34] C. 17, C. VII, q. 1; Jaffé, n. 2264.

[35] C. 5, X, *de clerico aegrotante vel debilitato,* III, 6; Potthast, n. 2335.

[36] C. un., *de clerico aegrotante vel debilitato,* III, 5, in VI°. Cf. Wernz-Vidal, *Ius Canonicum ad Codicis normam exactum,* Vol. II, *De Personis* (2 ed., Romae: apud Aedes Universitatis Gregorianae, 1928), p. 658. Hereinafter this will be cited *Ius Canonicum.*

[37] *Glossa Ordinaria* ad v. *non obstante* in c. un., *de clerico aegrotante vel debilitato,* III, 5, in VI°.

He argued that even in these instances the appointments were reserved to the Pope, for whom the recipients of the letters merely acted as delegates.[38] The same argument seems to apply also to the letter of Pope Gregory to Bishop Eleutherius. It should be noted, however, that this idea was in all probability not in the minds of the Roman Pontiffs as they delegated the power. This argument was used by Ioannes Andreae merely to show *post factum* that the law of Pope Boniface VIII was not inconsistent with previous legislation on this point.

However, it was realized that when a Coadjutor was necessary in a diocese from which, in view of its great distance from Rome, communication with the Holy See was difficult, the good of the diocese might demand an early choice of a Coadjutor. Pope Boniface therefore made provision for the choice of a Coadjutor when recourse to the Holy See entailed great inconvenience and when at the same time an appointment could not prudently be delayed. There were three possible instances for which the law provided, namely:

(1) when the Bishop himself wished to have a Coadjutor;

(2) when the Bishop was demented and hence was unable to express himself in the matter; and

(3) when the Bishop was opposed to the conferral of a Coadjutor.

In the first instance, when the Bishop recognized the need of a Coadjutor and was willing to accept this assistance, he was automatically empowered by law to appoint one or two Coadjutors after consulting the diocesan Chapter and obtaining the approval of a majority of its members.

Secondly, if the Bishop was demented or for any similar reason was unable to make a decision in the matter, then the Chapter was authorized by law to choose one or two Coadjutors. However, the consent of two-thirds of the members of the Chapter was required for this choice and decision. A majority vote which fell short of two-thirds did not suffice.[39] The Gloss on the words *auctoritate*

[38] *Glossa Ordinaria* ad v. *tantummodo,* in c. un., *de clerico aegrotante vel debilitato,* III, 5, in VI°.

[39] *Glossa Ordinaria* ad v. *duae ipsius partes* in c. un., X, *de clerico aegrotante vel debilitato,* III, 5, in VI°.

apostolica stated that the members of the Chapter acted as delegates of the Pope in this matter.

Lastly, if despite the evident need for a Coadjutor the Bishop was opposed to having one, and rejected the advice and request of his Chapter in the matter, the Chapter could not choose a Coadjutor against his will. But the Chapter was in such a case to report the condition of the Bishop and of his diocese to the Holy See. The decision of the Holy See was then to be awaited and accepted by all concerned.

It will be noted that in the foregoing ruling of Pope Boniface VIII the Bishop or, when the Bishop was incapacitated, the Chapter was allowed to choose two Coadjutors if this was deemed necessary. According to the Gloss on the words *aut duos,* more than two Coadjutors could not be chosen.[40]

Ioannes Andreae was of the opinion that one and the same Coadjutor could not be given to more than one Bishop.[41]

The Council of Trent (1545-1563) reiterated the rule of Pope Boniface VIII, namely, that the granting of a Coadjutor Bishop was reserved to the Roman Pontiff. However, the Council spoke only of that Coadjutor who had the right of future succession, and said nothing of the Coadjutor who was without this right. Moreover, nothing was said of the action that was to be taken by the Bishop or his Chapter in the various situations previously contemplated in the legislation of Pope Boniface VIII.[42] That legislation, not having been abrogated by any ecclesiastical authority, still remained in effect.

ARTICLE 4. TO WHOM A COADJUTOR WAS TO BE GRANTED

The reasons which were considered as justifying the granting of a Coadjutor to a Bishop were in general any disability which rendered the ruling Bishop permanently unable or unfit to fulfill the duties of his office. Pope Innocent III[43] and Pope Boniface VIII[44] gave the general rule that any "grave and incurable dis-

[40] C. un., *de clerico aegrotante vel debilitato,* III, 5, in VI°.

[41] *Novella,* Lib. III, tit. 6, c. 6, n. 13.

[42] Cf. sess. XXV, *de ref.* c. 7.

[43] C. 5, X, *de clerico aegrotante vel debilitato,* III, 6; Potthast, n. 2335.

[44] C. un., *de clerico aegrotante vel debilitato,* III, 5, in VI°; Potthast, n. 24311.

ease" which prevented the proper exercise of the episcopal office justified such an appointment. More specific examples given by Pope Boniface VIII were old age, bodily weakness and insanity.[45]

A ruling of Pope Lucius III (1181-1185), included in the Decretals of Pope Gregory IX, commanded that even a capable rector of any church who was afflicted with leprosy was to be given a Coadjutor in view of the danger that scandal to the faithful might otherwise be occasioned.[46]

The Gloss on the letter of Pope Innocent III to the Archbishop of Arles mentioned loss of eyesight[47] and loss of the power of speech[48] as reasons for the giving of a Coadjutor.

Rufinus (✠ *circa* 1190) in his commentary (*ca.* 1157-1159) on the letter of Pope Gregory I to the Deacon Anatolius at Constantinople treated the question of substituting one Bishop for another in a diocese, and taught that the incumbent Bishop could be forced to accept a substitute only if the disease he suffered was an incurable one. If the disease was curable, a substitute could be given only if he resigned. Moreover, if old age prevented him from exercising his duties, he could not be given a successor or a substitute, but only a Coadjutor.[49]

Both the letter of Pope Boniface VIII and that of Pope Innocent III, as mentioned above, dealt with Bishops who had incurable maladies. Later commentators on these texts extended the distinction of Rufinus with regard to a substitute for a Bishop, and applied it to the granting of Coadjutor Bishops. Ioannes Andreae[50] and Henricus Boich (ca. 1310-ca. 1350)[51] were of the opinion that, if the ailment was merely temporary, no Coadjutor was to be given. If, on the other hand, the impediment was perpetual, the granting of a Coadjutor was in order. Boich added that this rule obtained even in the case of leprosy.

---

[45] *Loc. cit.*

[46] C. 3, X, *de clerico aegrotante vel debilitato,* III, 6; Jaffé, n. 14965.

[47] *Glossa Ordinaria* ad v. *officium linguae* in c. 6, X, *de clerico aegrotante vel debilitato,* III, 6.

[48] *Casus,* in c. 6, X, *de clerico aegrotante vel debilitato,* III, 6.

[49] Rufinus, *Summa Decretorum* (ed. Heinrich Singer, Paderborn, 1902), in C. VII, q. 1 (p. 286).

[50] *Novella,* in c. 6, X, *de clerico aegrotante vel debilitato,* III, 6, n. 6.

[51] Lib. III, tit. 6, c. 6, n. 1.

Ioannes Andreae contended that an exiled Prelate was not to be given a Coadjutor, but rather a vicar was to be appointed to exercise his office.[52]

The Council of Trent stated simply that "urgent necessity or evident advantage" justified the appointment of a Coadjutor.[53]

ARTICLE 5. POWERS AND DUTIES OF THE COADJUTOR BISHOP

The tenor of the post-Gratian legislation and commentaries seems to imply that the Coadjutor Bishop had all of the powers and duties of the Bishop to whose diocese he was assigned, except for such limitations as the legislator saw fit to establish explicitly. Thus, Pope Boniface VIII, after giving directions concerning the appointment or election of a Coadjutor Bishop and defining certain limits of his power,[54] concluded by saying: "As for the rest, we wish and understand that what is stated (*praemittitur*) about Bishops is also to be referred to and applied in the case of higher prelates."[55] Moreover, the Gloss on the word *officium* of this text stated that it was the office of the Coadjutor to do whatever pertained to the office of the one to whom he was appointed.[56]

Although it has already been shown that Coadjutor Bishops were not considered Prelates in the strict sense, the writer is of the opinion that Pope Boniface VIII here referred to them as Prelates. The whole context of the passage indicates this, for previously the Pope had been discussing Coadjutors of Bishops. Therefore what applied to Bishops applied also to Coadjutor Bishops, unless the contrary was stated in a specific law or in the papal document appointing the Coadjutor.

The rule given by Pope Gregory I to Anatolius,[57] namely that the Coadjutor should "direct every care" of the Prelate who was

---

[52] *Loc. cit.*

[53] Conc. Trident., sess. XXV, *de ref.* c. 7.

[54] C. un., *de clerico aegrotante vel debilitato,* III, 5, in VI°.

[55] ". . . Ceterum quod de episcopis praemittitur, ad superiores etiam praelatos esse volumus et intelligimus referendum."—*Loc. cit.*

[56] *Glossa Ordinaria* ad v. *officium* in c. un., *de clerico aegrotante vel debilitato,* III, 5, in VI°.

[57] C. 1, C. VII, q. 1.

ill, was understood to mean that he should have "free and general administration" of the see.[58]

According to Ioannes Andreae the extent of the Coadjutor's powers was to be determined by the document of his appointment issued by the Holy See. If, however, he was appointed *simpliciter* (that is, for both spiritual and temporal matters in the diocese) he had all the powers of the Prelate to whom he was assigned, except for the alienation of immovables.[59] This latter restriction was based on the gloss of the letter of Pope Boniface VIII. The letter ruled that Coadjutors were to abstain from alienating the ecclesiastical goods of the Prelate.[60] The interpretation of the glossator implied that this restriction referred to all precious goods whether movable or immovable, but not to those movable goods which could not be preserved in their use.[61]

Ioannes Andreae discussed whether or not the conferral of benefices was among the powers of the Coadjutor. He distinguished three possible situations. First, if the Coadjutor was given for the administration of temporal matters only, the Bishop of the see retained the right to confer any benefice therein. (Ecclesiastical benefices were not included among the *temporalia.*)[62] Secondly, if the administration of the Coadjutor was to include spiritual matters, the Prelate nevertheless made the conferral, but the consent of the Coadjutor was required. Lastly, if the prelate was demented, the Coadjutor had power to confer benefices for him.[63]

Coadjutors were obliged to keep a strict account of their administration of the diocese, and Pope Boniface VIII ruled that

---

[58] *Glossa Ordinaria* ad v. *curam omnem* in c. 1, C. VII, q. 1.

[59] *Novella,* in c. 6, X, *de clerico aegrotante vel debilitato,* III, 6, n. 9; cf. also Pirhing, *Ius Canonicum, Nova Methodo Explicatum* (5 vols. in 4, Dilingae, 1674-1678), Lib. III, tit. 6, n. 16. Hereinafter this will be cited as Pirhing.

[60] C. un., *de clerico aegrotante vel debilitato,* III, 5, in VI°.

[61] *Glossa Ordinaria* ad v. *abstinentes* in c. un., *de clerico aegrotante vel debilitato,* III, 5, in VI°.

[62] *Glossa Ordinaria* ad v. *Coadiutorem* in c. 5, *de clerico aegrotante vel debilitato,* III, 6.

[63] *Novella,* in c. 6, X, *de clerico aegrotante vel debilitato,* III, 6, n. 9; cf. also Pirhing, Lib. III, tit. 6, n. 18.

they were to submit this account to the Bishop of the diocese and also to the members of the diocean Chapter. The successor of the Bishop could likewise call upon the Coadjutor for such an account, so that this provision was considered to have retroactive force.[64]

ARTICLE 6. SUPPORT OF THE COADJUTOR BISHOP

After a Coadjutor was appointed to a Bishop, he was to receive moderate support from the beneficial income which yielded to the incumbent Bishop.[65]

Pre-Tridentine commentators discussed the question: What is to be done if the income of the benefice is insufficient to support in a fitting manner both the Coadjutor and the Bishop to whom he was given? The Gloss on the word *portionem* presented an opinion which was contradicted by later commentators, namely, that in such an eventuality the Coadjutor was to have control of the income and from it support the ailing Bishop.[66]

Panormitanus cited this gloss, but disagreed with its doctrine. Ordinarily, he said, the needs of the infirm Prelate are to be satisfied and the remainder of the income is to be used as the Coadjutor shall direct. He proceeded to distinguish between the Coadjutor given *in spiritualibus* and the one given *in temporalibus.* In the former case the Prelate of the benefice directed the use of the income, and assigned a fitting portion of it to the Coadjutor. If the Coadjutor was given either *in temporalibus* or for both spiritual and temporal matters, the roles were reversed, the Coadjutor giving a suitable amount to the Prelate, likewise retaining a portion for himself and using the rest for the office with which he was charged. If it happened that the income of the benefice was not enough to provide for both the Coadjutor and the Prelate, the latter was to receive preference, and the obligation of sup-

---

[64] C. un., *de clerico aegrotante vel debilitato,* III, 5, in VI°.

[65] C. un., *de clerico aegrotante vel debilitato,* III, 5, in VI°; Ioannes Andreae, *Novella,* Lib. III, tit. 6, c. 6.

[66] *Glossa Ordinaria* ad v. *portionem* in c. 3, X, *de clerico aegrotante vel debilitato,* III, 6.

porting the Coadjutor then rested with the people of the diocese.[67]

Henricus Boich was of the opinion that when such a situation existed and the income of a cathedral benefice was insufficient, the matter was to be referred to the Holy See for settlement.[68]

The solution offered by the Council of Trent was to permit the conferral of a second benefice which helped to afford a sufficient income for the Coadjutor. This difficulty was considered by the Council as justification for an exception to the general rule which forbade the possession of more than one benefice. Even here, however, the second benefice conferred had to be one which did not require personal residence.[69]

ARTICLE 7. CESSATION FROM THE OFFICE OF COADJUTOR BISHOP

The office of the Coadjutor Bishop ended with the death of the Bishop to whom he was assigned, or by any other cause which ended the Prelate's term of office, such as renunciation or deposition. For, as Ioannes Andreae reasoned, upon the death of the one to whom the assignment had been made there was no longer anyone whom the Coadjutor could assist.[70]

The question of the cessation from office by Coadjutor Bishops who had the right of succession, or of their acquisition of title to the see upon the death of the ruling Bishop, was not discussed by pre-Tridentine authors. This was a comparatively late development, and hence will be treated in the following chapter.

---

[67] *Commentarium,* Lib. III, tit. 6, c. 3, nn. 5-6.

[68] Lib. III, tit. 6, c. 6.

[69] *Conc. Trident.,* sess. XXIV, *de ref.,* c. 17.

[70] *Novella,* Lib. III, tit. 6. c. 6.

CHAPTER III

Post-Tridentine Legislation

After the Council of Trent there was but little development in the office of the Coadjutor Bishop, either in the common law or in the discussions of the commentators. The opinions of the later commentators were substantially the same as those which prevailed among the pre-Tridentine authors regarding the various phases of the office considered in the preceding chapter. Consequently, what is there stated about Coadjutor Bishops constituted the prevailing opinion till the enactment of the Code of Canon Law in 1918.

Since the same knowledge and ability were always necessary for the office, it was hardly to be expected that anything more or less would be demanded in the matter of a candidate's qualifications than was indicated by pre-Tridentine authors.

The appointment of Coadjutor Bishops remained, as before the Council of Trent, one of the *causae maiores,* and therefore was reserved to the Roman Pontiff. However, the preliminary examination of the reasons for which the appointment of a Coadjutor Bishop was asked or proposed was made the work of the Congregation for the Erection of Churches and for Consistorial Provisions (the forerunner of the present Sacred Consistorial Congregation) by the Constitution *Immensa aeterni* of Pope Sixtus V (1585-1590) when he founded this Congregation on January 22, 1588.[1] The Constitution *Sapienti consilio* of Pius

[1] *Bullarum Diplomatum et Privilegiorum Sanctorum Romanorum Pontificum Taurinensis Editio* (24 vols. et Appendix, Neapoli, 1857-1872), VIII, 988: ". . . Quare aliam constituimus Cardinalium Congregationem, . . . Examinent praeterea . . . praesentationes, et nominationes, electionum sive postulationum confirmationes, seu admissiones, suffraganeorum coadiutorumque deputationes, cum futura successione, sive absque eadem successione...." Cf. Ferraris, *Prompta Bibliotheca canonica, juridica, moralis, theologica, necnon ascetica, polemica, rubricistica, historica* (8 vols., Petit-Montrouge, 1852), II, sub. v. "Congregationes," n. 6. Hereinafter this work will be cited as *Prompta Bibliotheca.* Cf. also Bouix, *Tractatus de Episcopo* (2 vols., Parisiis, 1859), I, 506.

X, reorganizing the Roman Curia in 1908, included among the offices of the Consistorial Congregation the election of Coadjutors and Auxiliaries of Bishops.[2]

Only two new phases of the office are of sufficient importance to merit special consideration here, namely:

(1) the introduction of the so called *Coadiutor perpetuus,* that is, the Coadjutor with the right of succession to a see; and

(2) the new prerogatives, powers and duties which became associated with the office of Coadjutor Bishops after the Council of Trent.

These phases will be considered in the following articles.

ARTICLE 1. THE COADJUTOR WITH THE RIGHT OF SUCCESSION

The reader will recall that in the first chapter of this historical survey mention was made of Pope Zachary's refusal in the year 748 to allow St. Boniface to appoint his successor except at the very hour of his death.[3] This attitude in opposition to the practice of having preappointed successors was reflected in the common law during the following centuries, not only in the matter of succession to episcopal sees, but in regard to all minor benefices as well.[4] The Council of Trent enacted a decree to this effect, reserving to the Holy See the appointment of all Coadjutors with the right of succession to benefices, whether episcopal in character or of a lesser degree.[5]

And so, as Pirhing (1606-1679) pointed out, the Coadjutorship with the right of succession was introduced, not by the common law, but by the practice of the Roman Curia, since such appoint-

---

[2] Pius X, const. *Sapienti consilio,* 29 iun. 1908, n. 2, 2:—"Adiutores et Auxiliarios Episcoporum eligere."—*Fontes,* n. 682.

[3] C. 17, C. VII, q. 1; Jaffé, n. 2264.

[4] C. 5, X, *de pactis,* I, 35; c. 2, X, *de concessione praebendae et ecclesiae non vacantis,* III, 8; c. 3, *de concessione praebendae et ecclesiae non vacantis,* III, 7, in VI°.

[5] *Conc. Trident.,* sess., XXV, *de ref.,* c. 7. Cf. Wernz, *Ius Decretalium* (6 vols., Romae et Prati: Ex Typographia Polyglotta, 1898-1905), II, *Ius Constitutionis Ecclesiae Catholicae,* n. 315. Hereinafter this will be cited as *Ius Decretalium.*

ments were often found expedient.[6] Fagnanus (1598-1678)[7] and Ferraris (✠ ca. 1763)[8] pointed to a decision of the Rota judge Cassadorus early in the sixteenth century as the first case concerning an appointment of a Coadjutor with the right of succession.

However, the introduction of the office of Coadjutor Bishops with the right of succession did not replace the office of temporary Coadjutor. Both offices existed under the law, and Coadjutors were appointed sometimes with, sometimes without, the right of succession.[9]

Pirhing stated that the Coadjutorship with the right of succession was not to be considered a benefice, for such a Coadjutor had only a *jus ad Prelaturam vel Beneficium,* and the benefice did not become vacant when the Coadjutor died during the lifetime of the Prelate whom he assisted.[10] Moreover, according to Ferraris, if a Coadjutor who was appointed with the right of succession became incapacitated so that he could not perform the duties of his office, he thereby lost the right of succession to the benefice.[11]

Both Coadjutorships, with or without the right of succession, ceased with the death of the ruling Bishop, but the *Coadjutor perpetuus* succeeded immediately to the benefice. As Fagnanus taught, the Coadjutor with the right of succession then had a full title to the benefice, whereas previously he had merely the *ius ad rem.*[12]

ARTICLE 2. POWERS AND DUTIES OF THE COADJUTOR BISHOP

Authors who wrote after the Council of Trent generally agreed with the opinions of the authors cited in the second chapter

[6] Pirhing, Lib. III, tit. 6, n. 20: "Huiusmodi autem Coadjutoriae non sunt Jure communi introductae, sed ex usu, more, ac stylo Curiae Romanae."

[7] *Commentaria in Quinque Libros Decretalium* (4 vols., Venetiis, 1696), Lib. III, tit. 6, n. 15. Hereinafter this work will be cited *Commentaria.*

[8] *Prompta Bibliotheca,* sub. v. "Coadjutor," n. 3.

[9] Ferraris, *Prompta Bibliotheca,* sub. v. "Coadjutor," n. 12.

[10] Pirhing, Lib. III, tit. 6, n. 21.

[11] *Prompta Bibliotheca,* sub. v. "Coadjutor," n. 86, citing the Rota decision *in Mindonien. Coadjutoriae,* Dec. 2, 1732, *coram Aldrovando.*

[12] *Commentaria,* II, Lib. III, tit. 6, n. 16.

concerning the powers and duties of Coadjutor Bishops. Such authors as Navarrus (Martinus de Azpilcueta, 1493-1587),[13] Nicolaus Garcias (✠ ca. 1613),[14] Piasecius (1578-1644),[15] Pirhing (1606-1679),[16] Reiffenstuel (1642-1703)[17] and Schmalzgrueber (1663-1735)[18] had little to add to the observations of pre-Tridentine writers.

The legislation on these matters is confined almost exclusively to applications of the general rules to particular cases by the Roman Congregations.

The Congregation of Bishops and Regulars declared on February 14, 1585, that the Coadjutor Bishop could not, without a special mandate from the Bishop, give a dispensation from the interstices required in the reception of Holy Orders.[19] Piasecius[20] cited a decree issued by the Sacred Congregation of Rites on January 31, 1591, which emphasized the subordination of the Coadjutor Bishop to his principal, even though he was a Coadjutor with the right of succession. He was forbidden to do anything which gave the impression of superiority over the ruling Bishop. For example, he could not enter the city *pontificaliter,* nor could he wear the pectoral cross (this being a sign of jurisdiction). Further, he was declared to have no faculty to grant indulgences independently of the ruling Bishop.

On September 30, 1596, the Sacred Congregation of Rites ruled that the Coadjutor Bishops of Verona and of Trent were

---

[13] *Omnia Opera* (6 vols., Venetiis, 1621), V, *Consiliorum in Quinque Libros et Titulos Decretalium Tomi Duo,* Lib. III, Concilium II. Hereinafter this work will be cited *Concilia.*

[14] *De Beneficiis* (Venetiis, 1618), Pars IV, c. 5.

[15] *Praxis Episcopalis, ea quae officium et potestatem Episcopi concernunt continens* (Coloniae Agrippinae, 1620), Proemium, n. 27. Hereinafter this will be cited *Praxis Episcopalis.*

[16] Pirhing, Lib. III, tit. 6, nn. 16 ff.

[17] *Jus Canonicum Universum* (5 vols. in 7, Parisiis, 1864-1870), III, tit. 6, nn. 49-54, et n. 61.

[18] *Jus Ecclesiasticum Universum* (5 vols. in 12, Romae, 1843-1845), V, tit. 6, nn. 25-29.

[19] Ferraris, *Prompta Bibliotheca,* sub. v. "Coadjutor," n. 78.

[20] *Loc. cit.*

entitled to take their place, in the order of their seniority of appointment to the episcopacy, among the other Bishops attending the Provincial Synod at Aquileia (*Aquileiensis*).[21]

Treating the question of the powers possessed by the Coadjutor in the absence of the principal, Navarrus[22] maintained that the Coadjutor could always act, even against the will of the absent principal, as long as he did not interfere in matters concerning the rule, administration or income of the benefice. Garcias[23] contradicted this opinion of Navarrus. He insisted that in the absence of the principal the Coadjutor could not act at all without permission.

It seems that the opinion of Navarrus, rather than that of Garcias, was upheld in a decision of the Congregation of Bishops and Regulars issued on May 13, 1603.[24] This ruling was given to a certain Bishop who complained that his Coadjutor was overstepping his authority in performing certain acts contrary to his wishes. It constitutes the origin of the present ruling in the Code of Canon Law that the Bishop should not habitually delegate to another what his Coadjutor can and is willing to perform.[25]

The Sacred Congregation ruled that when the Bishop was absent the Coadjutor did not need his permission to perform pontifical functions, since this was the precise reason for his appointment by the Pope. Furthermore, it was declared that in the present case the Coadjutor acted licitly in granting faculties for preaching. In fact, it was preferable that such faculties be granted by the Coadjutor, rather than by the vicar general. In 1623 the same Congregation issued another decree similar to that of 1603, stating that when a Bishop who has a Coadjutor is prevented

---

[21] S.R.C., *Aquileien.*, 30 sept. 1596—*Decreta Authentica Congregationis Sacrorum Rituum* (6 vols., Romae: ex Typographia Polyglotta, 1898-1927), I, n. 60. Hereinafter this will be cited as *Decr. Auth.* Cf. also *Codicis Iuris Canonici Fontes cura Emi Petri Card. Gasparri editi* (9 vols., Romae (postea civitate Vaticana): Typis Polyglottis Vaticanis, 1923-1939), n. 5176 for the text of this same decision. Hereinafter this will be cited *Fontes*.

[22] *Consilia*, Lib. III, tit. 6, Consilium II, n. 5.

[23] *De Beneficio*, Pars IV, cap. 5, nn. 58-60.

[24] S.C.Ep. et Reg., *Arianen.*, 13 maii 1603.—*Fontes*, n. 1619.

[25] Can. 351, § 3.

from exercising his office he cannot delegate his faculties to anyone except the Coadjutor.[26]

The Coadjutor Bishop was not obliged to make the visit *ad limina* as was the ruling Bishop, according to a decree issued by the Sacred Congregation of the Council on August 4, 1609.[27]

Another decree of the Congregation of Bishops and Regulars was to the effect that the Coadjutor Bishop should live at the residence of the Bishop and receive whatever was necessary for the exercise of his office.[28]

In reference to the duties of the Coadjutor Bishop the Congregation of Bishops and Regulars in 1628 answered a series of questions about which the Bishop of Foligno and his Coadjutor, the titular Bishop of Laodicaea, disputed.[29] A negative reply was given to the question whether the Coadjutor could be absent from the diocese of his appointment without permission of either the Bishop or the Sacred Congregation.[30] The Coadjutor was also obligated to perform all pontifical functions and other duties as requested by the ruling Bishop, even though the latter was in no way impeded from performing them himself.[31] Likewise the Coadjutor had to obey his Bishop when asked to accompany him on the diocesan visitation, but the expenses of the Coadjutor during the visitation had to be borne by the Bishop.[32] If the Bishop ordered the Coadjutor to make the diocesan visitation for him and assigned the vicar general to assist him, the Coadjutor could not refuse this assistance.[33]

---

[26] Ferraris, *Prompta Bibliotheca,* sub. v. "Coadjutor," n. 60, citing S.C.Ep. et Reg., in *Firmana,* 25 sept. 1623.

[27] Ferraris, *ibid.,* n. 56, citing S.C.C., 4 aug. 1609.

[28] S.C.Ep. et Reg., *Nicoteren.,* 7 sept. 1619—*Fontes,* n. 1704.

[29] S.C.Ep. et Reg., *Fulginaten.,* 26 maii 1628—*Fontes,* n. 1731.

[30] *Ibid.,* ad 1.

[31] *Ibid.,* ad 2.

[32] *Ibid.,* ad 5.

[33] *Ibid.,* ad ultimum.

PART II

CANONICAL COMMENTARY

CHAPTER IV

The Office of Coadjutor and Auxiliary Bishop in the Code of Canon Law

Article 1. Notion and Definition

Canon 350, § 2: Coadiutor dari solet personae Episcopi cum iure successionis; sed nonnumquam datur quoque sedi.

§ 3: Coadiutor, datus personae Episcopi sine iure successionis, speciali nomine dicitur *Auxiliaris*.

In canon 350 the Code mentions the threefold division of Coadjutors of Bishops. Two of these are said to be "given to the person of the Bishop" inasmuch as their Coadjutorship ordinarily continues only until the office of the residential Bishop to whom they are assigned expires. Their full titles, which are seldom used either in the Code or in the commentaries, are *Coadiutor datus personae Episcopi cum iure successionis,* or *Coadiutor datus personae Episcopi sine iure successionis,* according as they do or do not succeed to the rule of the diocese upon its vacancy. The Coadjutor to the person of the Bishop without the right of succession is also designated by the term *Auxiliaris.* The third type of Coadjutor is the *Coadiutor datus Sedi,* and he is so called inasmuch as his office does not cease with that of the principal Bishop but continues even during the vacancy of the See.

The Code states that it is customary for a Coadjutorship to be granted with the right of succession. This situation is not verified at the present time among the number of assistant Bishops in the United States, where the majority is without the right of succession to the See. Coadjutors assigned to the episcopal See itself are rare.[1] They are found in certain dioceses of Europe where because of a special privilege or immemorial custom sanctioned by the Holy See such appointments are continued.[2]

[1] Vermeersch-Creusen, *Epitome Iuris Canonici,* 2 ed. (3 vols., Mechliniae-Romae: H. Dessain, 1924), I, n. 419. Hereinafter this will be cited *Epitome.*

[2] Wernz, *Ius Decretalium,* II, n. 808.

The various definitions of Coadjutors of Bishops as listed by the authors may be summed up thus: They are those titular Bishops who are assigned by the authority of the Holy See to certain residential Bishops for the purpose of supplying their insufficiency or inability in the rule of the diocese or in the exercise of the episcopal power of orders.[3]

The *Coadiutor datus personae Episcopi,* with or without the right of succession, may be defined as that Coadjutor who is appointed to assist the resident Bishop in the exercise of episcopal *jurisdiction* as well as of the power of orders.[4] The *Coadiutor datus Sedi* is that Coadjutor who is appointed primarily to assist the resident Bishop in the exercise of the power of episcopal *orders* (confirmation, ordination, etc.).[5]

The essential difference between the *Coadiutor datus personae* and the *Coadiutor datus Sedi* should therefore be judged from the intention of the Holy See in making the appointment. The former is intended to help the resident Bishop in the exercise of the power of episcopal jurisdiction, the latter in the exercise of the episcopal power of orders. However, although this difference exists between these types of Coadjutors, there seems to be no reason why the characteristics of each Coadjutorship should not be combined in one and the same Coadjutor by the resident Bishop. Such action would not contradict the primary intention of the Holy See in making the appointment.

The foregoing statement seems reasonable in the light of Eichmann's[6] threefold division of Coadjutors: (1) Coadjutors given

[3] Coronata, *Institutiones Iuris Canonici* (5 vols., Taurini: Marietti, 1928-1936, Vol. I, 1928), I, n. 404; De Meester, *Juris Canonici et Juris Canonico-Civilis Compendium* (3 vols. in 4, Brugis: Desclée, 1921-1928, Vol. II, 1923), II, n. 704 (hereinafter cited *Compendium*); Sipos, *Enchiridion Iuris Canonici, ad usum scholarum* (Pécs: Ex Typographia "Haladás, R. J.," 1926), n. 51 (hereinafter cited *Enchiridion*).

[4] Chelodi, *Ius de Personis* (Tridenti: 2 ed. a Sac. Ernesto Bertagnolli Libr. Edit. Tridentum, 1927), n. 196 (b); cf. also Smith, *Elements of Ecclesiastical Law* (9 ed., 3 vols., New York: Benziger Bros., 1887-1888), I, n. 614; Wernz, *Ius Decretalium,* II, n. 810.

[5] Chelodi, *loc. cit.;* Smith, *op. cit.,* I, n. 613. Here Smith is defining "Auxiliary," a term used by pre-Code authors to designate the present office of *Coadiutor datus Sedi.*

[6] Eichmann, *Lehrbuch des Kirchenrechts auf Grund des Codex Iuris Canonici* (2 ed., Paderborn: Ferdinand Schoeningh, 1926), § 72 (1).

to the person of the Bishop with or without the right of succession; (2) Coadjutors given to the episcopal See; and (3) Coadjutors given simultaneously both to the person of the Bishop and to the See itself. According to Eichmann, then, the Holy See sometimes combines the features of both Coadjutorships in one man. In virtue of Canon 199, § 1, the resident Bishop can also do this if he sees fit, since he can delegate any or all of his powers of jurisdiction.[7]

To determine which kind of Coadjutor has been appointed by the Holy See in a particular instance, one must look first of all to the apostolic letter of appointment. That the document of appointment may not always be clear in this respect is seen from a question presented to the Sacred Consistorial Congregation in 1920. The Sacred Congregation was asked whether the Auxiliary Bishop of the Archdiocese of Managua was a *Coadiutor datus Sedi* or a *Coadiutor datus personae*. The reply was to the effect that the Auxiliary Bishop was given to the Archiepiscopal See, and not to the person of the Archbishop.[8]

It is to be noted that both the question presented and the response given refer to this *Coadiutor datus Sedi* as an "Auxiliary Bishop." The confusion of terminology here is probably only an apparent one. As will be pointed out presently, the term *Auxiliaris* among pre-Code authors did not have the same meaning that is now attached to it by the Code. The response of 1920 does not state when the Coadjutor Bishop of Managua was appointed However, it seems safe to assume that this appointment was made previous to the promulgation of the Code when the term *Auxiliaris* had the meaning now attached to the term *Coadiutor datus Sedi.* The difficulty may well have arisen because of this difference of terminology.

While it may be difficult at times to determine with certainty from the letters of appointment the type of Coadjutorship which

---

[7] Canon 199 § 1: "Qui iurisdictionis potestatem habet ordinariam, potest eam alteri ex toto vel ex parte delegare, nisi aliud expresse iure caveatur."

[8] Bouscaren, *The Canon Law Digest* (2 vols., Milwaukee: Bruce Publishing Company, 1934 and 1943), I, 211. Cf. *Acta Apostolicae Sedis, Commentarium Officiale* (Romae, 1909-), XII (1920), 41. Hereinafter this will be cited *AAS.*

is intended by the Holy See, some principles of guidance may be stated here. Primary consideration must be given the terminology in the document of appointment. Hence:

(1) If the document contains terms used by the Code to designate the office, these terms must be understood in the strict sense in which they are used by the Code. Thus, if the terms *Auxiliaris* or *Coadiutor datus Sedi* or *Coadiutor cum iure successionis* are used, there is no difficulty;

(2) if other terms equivalent to those in the Code (that is, terms found in post-Code commentaries) are used, they are to be taken in their commonly accepted sense;

(3) the *Coadiutor datus Sedi* seems to be indicated if the term *Auxiliaris* is not used and no mention is made of the right of succession, or if there is mention only of the exercise of the power of orders. A doubt regarding the appointment of a *Coadiutor datus Sedi* is unlikely to arise except in a diocese which customarily is granted such a *Coadjutor,* for example, in certain dioceses of Germany, Hungary, Portugal, Spain, or Italy.[9]

Should there be some doubt still remaining after these rules have been applied then it is possible that the circumstances under which the appointment was made will indicate the Holy See's intention. The reasons which usually prompt the Holy See to appoint the various types of Coadjutors will be considered in the next chapter. From the circumstances existing in the diocese previous to the time of the appointment of the assistant Bishop the intention of the Holy See may be conjectured. In this way a reasonable *modus agendi* can be determined until the Holy See can be asked for a decision in the matter.

Although all Coadjutors and Auxiliaries at the time of their appointment to assist a residential Bishop are made titular Bishops of ancient episcopal sees which have long ago fallen into desuetude as centers of Catholicity, the subject of titular Bishops as such is not within the scope of this dissertation. Not all titular Bishops are Coadjutor Bishops, for some are members of the Roman Curia or Papal Legates.[10] Any reference to titular Bishops

[9] Wernz-Vidal, *Ius Canonicum,* II, n. 616.

[10] Raus, *Institutiones Canonicae* (2 ed., Lugduni-Parisiis: Typis Emmanuelis Vitte, 1931), n. 131.

therefore will be made mainly in so far as it has a bearing on the subject of Coadjutor Bishops.

At one time titular Bishops were usually termed *"Episcopi in partibus infidelium,"* but Pope Leo XIII (1878-1903) ended this practice because many of the suppressed titular sees were no longer under the domination of infidels.[11]

For a clearer understanding of the concept of episcopal Coadjutorship there should be pointed out the difference between the office of Coadjutor and another office similar to it in many respects, that of the Apostolic Administrator. Coronata[12] lists the following differences between these two offices:

(1) A Coadjutor is always appointed to an occupied See, whereas the Administrator may be appointed either to a vacant or an occupied See.[13]

(2) The Administrator, during his term of office when the See is occupied, has all the jurisdictional powers of the Bishop, the power of the resident Bishop and his Vicar General being suspended.[14] This need not be and ordinarily is not so of a Coadjutor Bishop.

(3) Finally, the Coadjutor is appointed with a view to furnishing assistance for the residential Bishop; the Apostolic Administrator replaces the Bishop and assumes full responsibility in the care of the diocese.

Another difference, not mentioned by Coronata, is that Apostolic Administrators continue in office when the resident Bishop dies,[15] whereas a *Coadiutor datus personae* ceases from office.[16]

Despite these differences, the offices of Coadjutor Bishop and of Apostolic Administrator are not incompatible,[17] for sometimes a Coadjutor Bishop is also appointed the Administrator of a

---

[11] Wernz, *Ius Decretalium,* II, n. 808.

[12] *Institutiones Iuris Canonici,* I, n. 404.

[13] Can. 312.

[14] Can. 316, § 1.

[15] Can. 318.

[16] Can. 355.

[17] Can. 156, § 2: "Sunt incompatibilia officia quae una simul ab eodem adimpleri nequeunt."

diocese.[18] When this occurs it must be acknowledged that the appointee has all the rights and duties connected with each office, unless these are modified or augmented by the apostolic letter of appointment. At the death of the residential Bishop the Coadjutorship of an *Auxiliaris* would usually end, but he would continue to be the Apostolic Administrator.[19] A Coadjutor with the right of succession would become the residential Bishop[20] and thus cease to be either Coadjutor or Apostolic Administrator.

In the preceding paragraphs episcopal Coadjutorship has been consistently referred to as an ecclesiastical office. It is the contention of Wernz[21] (1842-1914) that an episcopal Coadjutorship as such is neither a benefice nor a Prelacy nor an ecclesiastical office. That it is not a benefice or a Prelacy is readily seen from the definitions of these terms in the Code. A benefice in the strict sense is a juridic entity permanently established by the competent ecclesiastical authority and consisting of a sacred office and the right to an income from an endowment annexed to the office.[22] Coadjutor Bishops are at times appointed to reserved benefices by the Holy See,[23] but ordinarily no endowed income is connected with a Coadjutorship, the support of the Coadjutor being provided by the principal Bishop. Any doubt about the beneficiary nature of a Coadjutorship is settled by Canon 1412, which states that whatever similarity a Coadjutorship with or without the right

---

[18] ". . . Sanctissimus Dominus Noster Pius Divina Providentia Pp. XII . . . per tramitem Sacrae Congregationis Consistorialis, Excmum et Revmum Dominum Leonem Binz . . . eundemque deputavit in munus Episcopi Coadiutoris Excmi et Revmi D. Francisci M. Kelly, Episcopi Winonensis, cum iure in eandem sedem Winonensem futurae successionis, atque insuper cum titulo, iuribus, honoribus et obligationibus Administratoris Apostolici, ad normam Canonis 315, § 1. . . ."—Original document of appointment of the Most Rev. Leo Binz, Apostolic Administrator and Coadjutor Bishop with the right of future succession in the diocese of Winona.

[19] Cans. 318, § 1, and 355, § 2.

[20] Can. 355, § 1.

[21] *Ius Decretalium,* II, n. 810 (I).

[22] Can. 1409.

[23] Can. 1433.

of succession may bear to true benefices, it is not to be classified as a benefice.[24]

It is also true that a Coadjutorship is not a Prelacy in the strict sense. Although the term *Praelatus* often refers to merely honorary positions (such as "domestic prelates"), it is commonly used in the Code to describe clerics whose office gives them some ordinary power of jurisdiction in the external forum.[25] As will be seen, Coadjutors ordinarily do not have such power by the mere fact of their appointment. Hence they may be, and often are, referred to as prelates, but only in the wide sense.

However, the question whether the Coadjutorship as such is an ecclesiastical office in the strict sense is not as easily decided as the questions of benefice and Prelacy. In the wide sense of the term an ecclesiastical office is any duty performed for a spiritual end,[26] and this certainly applies to any Coadjutorship. But in the strict sense an ecclesiastical office has these three elements:[27]

(1) it must be permanently established by divine or ecclesiastical authority;

(2) it must be conferred according to specific rules of the Code; and

(3) it must partake of the ecclesiastical power of orders or of jurisdiction.

The first two conditions offer no difficulty. For many centuries the position of Coadjutor Bishop has been, and now continues to be, the subject of Church legislation. Further, the rules governing the method of appointment are practically the same as those for the appointment of residential Bishops.

In regard to the third condition mentioned above, a controversy exists as to whether the ecclesiastical power required by Canon 145 must be ordinary or whether merely delegated power suffices.

The main difficulty in settling this problem is not in finding arguments to support one side or the other, but rather, having chosen one side, how to reconcile one's view with the arguments to the contrary. The question is only an incidental one in this dissertation, but it is essential to McDevitt's work on "The Renuncia-

[24] Can. 1412: Licet aliquam cum beneficiis similitudinem praeseferant, in iure tamen beneficii nomine non veniunt: . . .

3°—Coadiutoriae cum vel sine futura successione;

[25] Can. 110.

[26] Can. 145, § 1.

[27] *Ibid.*

tion of An Ecclesiastical Office."[28] McDevitt cites authors who hold opposing views on the question whether an ecclesiastical office in the strict sense must have ordinary power, or whether delegated power is sufficient.[29] Without attempting to settle the dispute, he says merely that he prefers the view which holds that ordinary power is necessary. However, the present writer prefers the view that delegated power suffices for a strict ecclesiastical office for the following reasons:

(1) Canon 145 does not specify that ordinary power is necessary for a strict ecclesiastical office.

(2) The same canon states that when the term *ecclesiasticum officium* is used in the Code, it is to be understood in the strict sense unless the contrary is evident from the context.

(3) The term *officium* is used in reference to Coadjutors and Auxiliaries of Bishops in Canons 353, § 1, and 355, §§ 2 and 3, and it is by no means apparent from the context that an ecclesiastical office in the wide sense is to be understood.

(4) As will be seen, of the three types of Coadjutor Bishops only the *Coadiutor datus Sedi* has ordinary power, not of jurisdiction but of orders. Otherwise, Coadjutor Bishops have no ordinary power, whether of orders or of jurisdiction, by the mere fact of their appointment.

McDevitt[30] states that Coadjutor Bishops have an ecclesiastical office in the strict sense because they have the right to exercise pontifical orders, with the exception of ordinations, in the diocese of their appointment. However, this is true only of the *Coadiutor datus Sedi.*

ARTICLE 2. TERMINOLOGY

While the notion of all three types of Coadjutorship existed in canonical legislation and commentaries previous to the promulgation of the Code, the terminology used to designate them differed

---

[28] The Catholic University of America Canon Law Studies, n. 218 (Washington, D. C.: The Catholic University of America Press, 1946).

[29] *Op. cit.*, pp. 4-6.

[30] *Op. cit.*, p. 5.

considerably from that of the Code in canons 350-355, and of the commentaries written since 1917. Pre-Code authors generally divided assistant Bishops into two categories called *Vicarii in pontificalibus* (or "Auxiliaries") and *Coadiutores,* including under the latter term those with and without the right of future succession.[31]

Terms designating the present *Coadiutor datus personae Episcopi cum iure successionis* are much the same in legislation and commentaries before and since the promulgation of the Code. The most common are the abbreviated forms, *Coadiutor cum iure successionis*[32] and *Coadiutor cum futura successione.*[33] The term *Coadiutor perpetuus,* as used by Wernz,[34] is retained by Vidal.[35] Since the Coadjutorship with the right of succession is the one customarily granted, the incumbent is often referred to as the *Coadiutor proprie dictus.*[36]

The term *Auxiliaris* now used in the Code has a technical meaning entirely different from the same term as used by the pre-Code authors.[37] A reading of these authors shows that their use of the term is practically synonymous with the present term *Coadiutor datus Sedi.*[38] As the Code states, the word *Auxiliaris* now refers exclusively to the *Coadiutor datus personae* who has not the right of future succession to the See. Henceforth any use of the term in documents issued by the Holy See or in commentaries must be presumed to have this special meaning.

---

[31] Wernz, *Ius Decretalium,* II, nn. 808-809; Smith, *Elements of Ecclesiastical Law,* I, nn. 613-614.

[32] Can. 355, § 1; Bargilliat, *Praelectiones Juris Canonici* (37 ed., 2 vols., Parisiis: apud Baston, Berche et Pagis, 1923), I, n. 784.

[33] Cans. 353, § 2, and 1433; Wernz, *Ius Decretalium,* II, n. 810.

[34] Wernz, *Ius Decretalium,* II, n. 810.

[35] Wernz-Vidal, *Ius Canonicum,* II, n. 617.

[36] Raus, *Institutiones Canonicae,* n. 131.

[37] "Auxiliares vocabantur quoque Vicarii in pontificalibus vel etiam suffraganei; hoc nomen nunc alium omnino sensum habet."—Vermeersch-Creusen, *Epitome,* I, n. 419.

[38] Cf. Smith, *Elements of Ecclesiastical Law,* I, n. 613: "Auxiliary Bishops (episcopi suffraganei, vicarii in pontificalibus) are titular Bishops appointed by the Holy See to assist ordinary Bishops, not in the exercise of their jurisdiction, but merely of the *ordo episcopalis,* e.g., to give confirmation."

Just as the Coadjutor with the right of succession is sometimes called *Coadiutor perpetuus,* so the correlative term *Coadiutor temporalis* is sometimes found in reference to the one without the right of future succession to the See.[39] *Coadiutor sine iure successionis*[40] and *Coadiutor sine futura successione*[41] are other terms often applied to this type of Coadjutorship.

The term *Coadiutor datus Sedi* now appearing in the Code was not used by pre-Code authors. These Coadjutors were most frequently referred to as *Vicarii in pontificalibus.*[42] The reason for this usage was the fact that their duties as Bishops were for the most part concerned with the exercise of the episcopal power of orders. As has already been mentioned they were also called *Auxiliares.*[43] Vidal refers to them as *"Auxiliares seu Vicarii in pontificalibus."*[44] Less common but often used to describe these Coadjutors was the term *Suffraganeus.* However, while most pre-Code authors applied this term to the present *Coadiutor datus Sedi,*[45] Sebastianelli (✠ 1920) gives an entirely different twofold meaning to *suffraganeus.* He says that it may refer to any Coadjutor given to a Bishop who is also a Cardinal. The second meaning of *suffraganeus* according to this same author is the meaning usually attached to it today, namely, a Bishop subject to the Metropolitan of a province.[46]

Whenever the term *Coadiutor* stands alone without any modifier in Church legislation, as in Canons 338 and 342, it is understood to refer equally to all three types of Coadjutors. Likewise, unless otherwise stated or evident from the context, all references to Coadjutors in the following pages will be applicable to all alike.

The residential Bishop to whom a Coadjutor is given is sometimes referred to as the *Coadiutus.*[47]

---

[39] Wernz, *Ius Decretalium,* II, n. 810; Smith, *Elements of Ecclesiastical Law,* I, n. 614; Wernz-Vidal, *Ius Canonicum,* II, n. 617.

[40] Chelodi, *Ius de Personis,* n. 196.

[41] Canon 1433.

[42] Wernz, *Ius Decretalium,* II, nn. 807-808.

[43] Smith, *Elements of Ecclesiastical* Law, I, n. 613.

[44] Wernz-Vidal, *Ius Canonicum,* I, n. 616.

[45] Wernz, *Ius Decretalium,* II, n. 808.

[46] Sebastianelli, *Praelectiones Juris Canonici—De Personis* (2 ed., Romae: Fredericus Pustet, 1905), p. 230.

[47] Can. 354.

CHAPTER V

Canonical Appointment of Coadjutor Bishops

ARTICLE 1. RESERVATION OF THE APPOINTMENT TO THE HOLY SEE

Canon 350, § 1: Unius Romani Pontificis est Episcopo Coadiutorem constituere.

As before the promulgation of the Code of Canon Law, so now the appointment of Coadjutors and Auxiliaries of Bishops is considered a *causa maior,* and hence is reserved to the Holy See.[1] The same formalities are observed in choosing Coadjutors as in the choice of residential Bishops.[2]

In general there are five ways in which ecclesiastical offices may be conferred:[3]

(1) through a free bestowal on the part of the proper ecclesiastical superior (*libera collatio*);

(2) through appointment by the lawful superior after presentation of the candidate by one having such a right (*institutio*);

(3) through the superior's confirmation of an elected candidate;

(4) through permission of the competent Superior in favor of a candidate, otherwise barred from office by an impediment, to accept the office after he has received the vote of postulation[4] (*admissio*);

(5) through election alone, when the law does not demand confirmation of it.

By far the most common method of appointing Coadjutors and Auxiliaries of Bishops is the so called free bestowal. In view of

---

[1] Cf. can. 220; Beste, *Introductio in Codicem* (2 ed., Collegeville, Minn.: St. John's Abbey Press, 1944), p. 272; Wernz, *Ius Decretalium,* II, n. 808 (d); Sipos, *Enchiridion,* n. 51.

[2] Beste, *loc. cit.*

[3] Can. 148, § 1.

[4] Can. 179.

canon 350, § 1, it may be asked whether any other method, such as election or presentation of the candidate, is possible. The Pope, by reason of his primacy of jurisdiction over the universal Church has free power to confer any ecclesiastical office.[5] This power is exercised especially in the choice of Bishops.[6] However, canon 350, § 1, is not to be interpreted so strictly as to deny any possibility of election or nomination of Coadjutor Bishops, since the correlative rule about the appointment of residential Bishops, as enacted in canon 329, § 2,[7] admits of such exceptions. But it must be remembered that, if the right to elect or nominate a Bishop is had by a Chapter or civil government, the source of this power is to be found in a special right or privilege granted by the Holy See.[8]

The question of the right to elect or nominate Coadjutors and Auxiliaries of Bishops may be stated as follows: Where a diocesan Chapter has the right to elect, or a civil government has the right to nominate, the residential Bishop of a diocese, does this right also obtain when there is question of appointing a Coadjutor Bishop to that diocese? Authors are not at one in their answers. Some deny the extension of this right to the election or nomination of Coadjutors, while others affirm it. Still others limit this extension to the election or nomination of Coadjutors with the right of succession. But despite the difference of views among the authors, the disagreement is not as great as a cursory reading of the texts might lead one to believe. Even those who uphold the right of the Chapter or civil government seem to agree that no one has a strict right to nominate or elect a Coadjutor of any kind, even if the right to nominate the residential Bishop is had. The privilege of nominating a Coadjutor is only a further concession given at times, but which the Holy See is by no means obliged to give.

---

[5] Wernz-Vidal, *Ius canonicum,* II, n. 225.

[6] Can. 329.

[7] Can. 329, § 2. "Eos [Episcopos] libere nominat Romanus Pontifex.

§ 3 Si cui collegio concessum sit ius eligendi Episcopum, servetur praescriptum can. 321.

[8] Can. 332, § 1; Wernz-Vidal, *op. cit.,* II, n. 230.

Ayrinhac (1867-1930)[9] and Vidal[10] stated that no Coadjutor Bishop can be elected by a Chapter or nominated by a civil government even if the right to elect or nominate the residential Bishop is had. Vidal qualifies this however by saying that the practice of the Holy See shows that this is not allowed unless it be expressly granted through an apostolic indult. Coronata[11] and Wernz[12] took the opposite position, claiming that whenever any Coadjutor Bishop is to be appointed the Holy See should take into consideration the right of those who have the right to elect or nominate the residential Bishop.

However, most of the authors[13] who treat this point maintain that the Holy See should consult the Chapter or civil government when the Coadjutor to be appointed will have the right of succession. They imply that such consultation is not necessary when any other type of Coadjutorship is being considered. To the present writer this opinion appears to be the most tenable, for the appointment of a *Coadiutor cum iure successionis* is equivalent to the appointment of the next residential Bishop of the diocese, whereas this would not be so of the appointment of any other type of Coadjutor.

Sipos[14] states that the civil government with the right of nomination should always be consulted regarding the appointment of a *Coadiutor cum iure successionis,* but that the consent of the Chapter is not necessary at any time. Augustine (1872-1943)[15] mentioned only the right of the Chapter in such a case. He also pointed out that in the United States there are no elections of Bishops by the Chapter (or consultors). The same is true of the nomination of Bishops by the civil government.

---

[9] *The Constitution of the Church in the New Code of Canon Law* (New York: Blase Benziger, 1925), n. 152. This author cites Wernz as authority for his view. Wernz however does not seem to support his contention.

[10] Wernz-Vidal, *Ius canonicum,* II, n. 616 (I).

[11] *Institutiones Iuris Canonici,* I, n. 405.

[12] *Ius Decretalium,* II, n. 810.

[13] Bargilliat, *Praelectiones Juris Canonici,* I, n. 785; Beste, *Introductio in Codicem,* p. 272; Chelodi, *Ius de Personis,* n. 196; Vermeersch-Creusen, *Epitome,* I, n. 420.

[14] *Enchiridion,* n. 51.

[15] *A Commentary on the New Code of Canon Law* (8 vols., St. Louis: B. Herder, 1925-1938, Vol. II, 6 ed., 1936), II, 380.

It often happens, of course, that such difficulties between the civil government and the Holy See are obviated by provisions made in concordats concerning the right of consultation or nomination upon the appointment of Coadjutor Bishops in certain countries. When the right to nominate Bishops is had by a civil government, the Holy See invariably extends this right to the nomination of Coadjutor Bishops with the right of succession.[16]

Apart from such exceptional instances of the election or presentation of candidates, the usual conferral of Coadjutorships, as in the case of residential Bishops, takes place through the process of free bestowal by the Holy See.[17] In this process of the free bestowal of a Coadjutorship there are ordinarily three phases:[18]

(1) The choice of the person for the Coadjutorship;

(2) The appointment of the Coadjutor;

(3) The act of taking office by the one appointed.

Strictly considered, both the choice and the appointment of Bishops are made by the Roman Pontiff through the Sacred Consistorial Congregation[19] or the Congregation for the Propagation of the Faith.[20] However, it is the practice of the Holy See to request the heirarchy in various countries of the world, especially those more distant from Rome, to recommend candidates for the episcopacy. By this means the Sacred Congregation is able to find worthy candidates, determine their qualifications, and decide who among these candidates would be best able to accomplish the work to be done in a particular episcopal See. To expedite this presentation of candidates, the Sacred Consistorial Congregation has issued special instructions to be observed in the choice of candidates by the Bishops in certain countries.

Such an instruction for the hierarchy of the United States ap-

---

[16] Cf. Polish Concordat, Art. XI: *AAS,* XVII (1925), 277; Lithuanian Concordat, Art. XI: *AAS,* XIX (1927), 428; German Concordat, Art. XIV, 2: *AAS,* XXV (1933), 397; Austrian Concordat, Art. IV, § 2: *AAS,* XXVI (1934), 253.

[17] Sipos, *Enchiridion,* n. 51; Wernz, *Ius Decretalium,* II, n. 808 (d).

[18] Wernz-Vidal, *Ius Canonicum,* II, n. 182.

[19] Can. 248, § 2.

[20] Can. 252, § 1, and § 3, and can. 248, § 2.

peared in 1916.[21] Presumably it applies to the presentation of candidates for Coadjutorships as well as of residential Bishops, since no distinction is made in the instruction. At the outset it is stated that the former method outlined by the III Plenary Council of Baltimore (1884)[22] is no longer adapted to the situation in this country.[23] Hereafter, at the beginning of Lent in each odd-numbered year, every Bishop is to present to the Metropolitan the names of two priests whom he considers worthy of the episcopacy. Presumably Coadjutor Bishops have the right to present names of candidates since the instruction says that this is to be done by all the Bishops of the Province. The Archbishop, having received the names, adds two more names of his own choice, and has a list arranged alphabetically without mentioning the names of the Bishops by whom the candidates were nominated. This is sent to the suffragan Bishops who are to investigate the qualifications of those listed who are not personally known to them.

Sometime after Easter the Archbishop is to call an informal meeting of the Bishops at which the merits of the candidates are discussed and a secret vote is taken. The results of the voting and a copy of the complete proceedings of the meeting are forwarded to the Sacred Consistorial Congregation. The Bishops may also make any recommendations which may influence the Holy See in appointing someone to a particular diocese. All the foregoing

[21] S.C.Consist., decr. 25 iul. 1916—*AAS,* VIII (1916), 400-404. Decrees issued for other countries are: Canada and Newfoundland—S.C.Consist., decr. 19 mart. 1919—*AAS,* XI (1919), 124-128; Scotland—S.C.Consist., decr. 20 nov. 1920—*AAS,* XIII (1921), 13-16; Brazil—S.C.Consist., decr. 19 mart. 1921—*AAS,* XIII (1921), 222-225; Mexico—S.C.Consist., decr. 30 apr. 1921—*AAS,* XIII (1921), 379-382; Poland (Latin Rite)—S.C.Consist., decr. 20 aug. 1921—*AAS,* XIII (1921), 430-432. Cf. Bouscaren, *The Canon Law Digest,* I, 194-198.

[22] *Acta et Decreta Concilii Plenarii Baltimorensis Tertii A. D. MDCCCLXXXIV* (Baltimorae: Typis Ioannis Murphy Sociorum, 1886), n. 15.

[23] "Ratio pro candidatis ad episcopale ministerium proponendis, quae in istis Foederatis Americae Statibus viget, . . . quamvis iteratis Baltimorensis Concilii studiis et S. Sedis provisionibus, melior sensim evaserit, praesentibus tamen Ecclesiae necessitatibus non videtur plene respondere."—*AAS,* VIII (1916) 400.

nominations, investigations and voting are to be executed as inconspicuously as possible, and the Bishops are placed under an oath of secrecy regarding the discussions of the meeting.

Thus the Holy See has always at hand a list of priests worthy of promotion to the episcopacy whenever it is necessary to appoint a residential Bishop or a Coadjutor. In the appointment of a Coadjutor Bishop, however, the Holy See usually considers not only the recommendation of the Bishops of a province or country, but also the wishes of the residential Bishop whom the one appointed will assist, should he desire some particular priest as his Coadjutor.[24] Hence, if the residential Bishop thinks there is need of a Coadjutor in the diocese he may request the Holy See to appoint one, and he may name the priest he prefers. But while this is customary in the appointment of Coadjutors, there is nothing to prevent the Holy See either from appointing a Coadjutor against the will of the resident Bishop, or from naming for the position someone other than the priest requested by him, should such action seem advisable or necessary.[25]

As canon 350, § 1, states, it is the Pope alone who appoints Coadjutor Bishops, but he does so only after the investigation of the candidate's qualifications. The performance of the acts preliminary to the appointment is one of the duties of the Sacred Consistorial Congregation,[26] except in cases where the Coadjutor is to be appointed for a territory subject to the Congregation for the Propagation of the Faith.[27] The Pope makes the appointment on the recommendation of the proper Congregation.

In the historical part of this dissertation consideration was given to the difficulty which sometimes arose previous to the

---

[24] Coronata, *Institutiones Iuris Canonici,* I, n. 405; Sipos, *Enchiridion,* n. 51; Smith, *Elements of Ecclesiastical Law,* I, n. 615; Wernz, *Ius Decretalium,* II, nn. 808 and 810; Beste, *Introductio in Codicem,* p. 272.

[25] Smith, *loc. cit.;* Wernz, *op. cit.,* II, n. 810 (II).

[26] Can. 248, § 2. Cf. Wernz, *op. cit.,* II, n. 808; Blat, *Commentarium Textus Codicis Iuris Canonici* (6 vols., Romae: Libreria del Collegio Angelico, 1919-1927), II, 320. Hereinafter this work will be cited *Commentarium.*

[27] Cans. 248, § 2, and 252; Wernz, *loc. cit.;* Wernz-Vidal, *Ius Canonicum,* II, n. 617.

promulgation of the Code in dioceses distant from Rome where a Coadjutor was needed, but time did not allow consultation of the Holy See.[28] This difficulty was of practical importance even towards the close of the last century.[29] Today, however, with the ease of communication in transmitting messages to the Holy See, such situations rarely if ever occur. Consequently the legislation occasioned by this difficulty is no longer in force.[30] Neither the residential Bishop nor the Cathedral Chapter (nor the diocesan consultors) can now appoint a Coadjutor Bishop under any circumstances. The need for one must in every case be reported to the Holy See.

As required by the Council of Trent,[31] so today any Coadjutor Bishop must have the same qualifications that are necessary for residential Bishops.[32] Therefore he must be at least thirty years of age, at least five years in the priesthood and of legitimate birth, not merely legitimated. He must have the qualities of character and ability which will best fit him to fulfill the duties that will be his in the diocese of his assignment, and he should moreover be learned in the sciences of Theology and of Canon Law.[33]

Sipos[34] states that a Coadjutor is usually a Bishop, thus implying that he need not necessarily be one. In the latter case, according to Wernz,[35] the law specifies nothing concerning his qualifications, but they should be at least equal to those expected of a Vicar General or a Vicar Capitular.[36]

The circumstances in a diocese which prompt the Holy See to appoint a Coadjutor Bishop vary in the three types of Coadjutorship. In dioceses where it is customary for the Holy See to appoint

---

[28] *Supra*, p. 19.

[29] Smith, *Elements of Ecclesiastical Law*, I, n. 615.

[30] Wernz-Vidal, *Ius Canonicum*, II, n. 616 (I); Blat, *Commentarium*, II, 320.

[31] Sess. XXV, *de ref.* c. 7; cf. *supra*, p. 18.

[32] Bargilliat, *Praelectiones Juris Canonici*, I, n. 785; Wernz, *Ius Decretalium*, II, n. 810 (II).

[33] Can. 331, § 1.

[34] *Enchiridion*, n. 51.

[35] *Ius Decretalium*, II, n. 810 (II).

[36] Cf. cans. 367 and 434.

a *Coadiutor datus Sedi,* the usual reason is that the diocese is so large, either in territory or in the number of the faithful, that the principal Bishop alone, even though he be capable and in good health, cannot do everything required of him in the exercise of the power of episcopal orders and jurisdiction. The *Coadiutor datus Sedi* is appointed to relieve him completely or in part of the duties requiring the power of episcopal orders.[37]

In assigning reasons for the appointment of a *Coadiutor datus personae Episcopi* few authors distinguish between those with and those without the right of succession. Most of the reasons assigned for either type of Coadjutorship concern the ill health of the residential Bishop—for example, old age, chronic or incurable disease, loss of speech, blindness and insanity.[38] Other reasons advanced are the dignity of the one given the Coadjutor (e.g., a Cardinal or Archbishop),[39] large population or area of the diocese,[40] or inefficient management on the part of the principal Bishop.[41]

The designation of a *Coadiutor cum iure successionis* is usually occasioned by more weighty reasons than that of an *Auxiliaris.*[42] The traditional aversion to the appointment of a successor to an office before its vacancy[43] was overcome only gradually as the need for such Coadjutor Bishops became more evident.[44] At times it may be deemed advisable to forestall a long vacancy in view of the special needs of the diocese, or to obviate an impending danger of discord among the officials of the diocese through an

---

[37] Chelodi, *Ius de Personis,* n. 196; Coronata, *Institutiones Iuris Canonici,* I, n. 404; Smith, *Elements of Ecclesiastical Law,* I, n. 613; Beste, *Introductio in Codicem,* p. 272.

[38] Ayrinhac, *The Constitution of the Church,* n. 153; Smith, *op. cit.,* I, n. 615; Beste, *Introductio in Codicem,* p. 272; Vermeersch-Creusen, *Epitome,* I, n. 419 (2).

[39] Beste, *loc. cit.*

[40] Vermeersch-Creusen, *loc. cit.*

[41] Smith, *loc. cit.*

[42] Wernz, *Ius Decretalium,* II, n. 810; Wernz-Vidal, *Ius Canonicum,* II, n. 617.

[43] Cf. *supra,* p. 27.

[44] Smith, *op. cit.,* I, n. 614.

anticipated naming of the future Ordinary.[45] A Coadjutor with the right of succession will now be chosen rather than an *Auxiliaris* whenever this choice seems the better policy for the good of the diocese.[46]

ARTICLE 2. THE ACT OF TAKING OFFICE

Canon 353, § 1: Quilibet Coadiutor, ut canonicam sui officii possessionem capiat, necesse est litteras apostolicas ostendat Episcopo.

§ 2: Coadiutor cum futura successione et Coadiutor sedi datus debent praeterea easdem ostendere Capitulo ad normam can. 334, § 3.

§ 3: Si Episcopus eum in statum inciderit ut eliciendi actus humani sit impos, praetermisso praescripto § 1, solum praescriptum § 2 ab omnibus Coadiutoribus servetur.

Except for the special rules enacted in the just-quoted canon, the laws governing the taking of office by Coadjutor Bishops are practically the same as the ones to be observed by those who are appointed as residential Bishops.[47] Hence, if he is not a Bishop at the time of his appointment, the Coadjutor must receive the episcopal consecration within three months from the time that the official letter of appointment has reached him.[48] He must also report to the diocese of his appointment within four months after the reception of the letter of appointment.[49]

Usually the consecration of the Bishop takes place before the act of possession of office, but this need not be so.[50] Therefore a Coadjutor can take possession of his office before or after his consecration. If necessary, he may also take possession of his office by proxy.[51] If the sending of the apostolic letter has been delayed (e.g., in time of war), it suffices for the appointee to

---

[45] Wernz-Vidal, *loc. cit.*

[46] Wernz, *loc. cit.;* Wernz-Vidal, *loc. cit.*

[47] Cf. cans. 332 to 334.

[48] Can. 333.

[49] Can. 333.

[50] Wernz-Vidal, *Ius Canonicum,* II, n. 597.

[51] Can. 334, § 3.

present an authentic notification of his promotion as Coadjutor. A Coadjutor who is appointed a titular Archbishop need not seek the pallium, since the pallium symbolizes ordinary Archiepiscopal jurisdiction.[52]

In the canons dealing directly with Coadjutor Bishops nothing is said of the profession of faith or the oath of loyalty to the Holy See, but canon 332, § 2, prescribes them for all Bishops before they take their office. The penalty for failure to make the profession of faith is severe, and may even include deprivation of office.[53] It is to be made in person, not by proxy.[54] However, it seems that any failure to make the profession of faith does not invalidate the act of taking office, for canon 2403 speaks of deprivation of office for such failure, thus implying that the office has been validly held previous to the deprivation.

The possession of office by Coadjutor Bishops is effected by the presentation of the apostolic letter of appointment to the proper authority. Ordinarily all Coadjutors must show the apostolic letter to the residential Bishop. The *Auxiliaris* needs to present them to no one else. The *Coadiutor datus Sedi* and the Coadjutor with the right of succession must present them to the Cathedral Chapter as well as to the residential Bishop. In the dioceses of the United States and in all dioceses not having a Cathedral Chapter the diocesan consultors take the place of the Chapter,[55] and the apostolic letter must correspondingly be presented to them.[56] In executing this formality it does not suffice to present the letter to the members of the Chapter individually, but rather all the members must be convoked for this purpose, and the chancellor must be present to record it.[57]

If at the time of the presentation of the apostolic letter the residential Bishop is, as the Code says, unable to place a human act, then all Coadjutor Bishops take possession of their office merely by showing the apostolic letter to the Cathedral Chapter

[52] Wernz, *Ius Decretalium,* II, n. 808; cf. also can. 275.

[53] Can. 2403.

[54] Can. 1407.

[55] Can. 427.

[56] Augustine, *A Commentary on the New Code of Canon Law,* II, p. 382.

[57] Beste, *Introductio in Codicem,* p. 267.

or the diocesan consultors. In other words, this can be done whenever the residential Bishop is so incapacitated that he cannot understand the meaning of the ceremony.[58] It is not necessary that the Bishop be incapacitated permanently or for a long time. Even if it is apparent that the residential Bishop will very soon recover from his infirmity, there is no obligation to delay the taking of office until his recovery. Nor is it necessary for the validity of the act of possession that the Coadjutor afterward show the apostolic letter to the residential Bishop.

But if the residential Bishop has been taken ill and it seems certain that he will soon die, should the Coadjutor proceed to take possession of his office? In answer to this question it is necessary to distinguish between the three types of Coadjutorship. Since the *Coadiutor datus Sedi* does not depend on the residential Bishop for his tenure of office, but continues in office even during the vacancy of the See, there seems to be no reason why he should not proceed to the possession of the office. Similarly, in the case of the Coadjutor with the right of succession, since the apparent intention of the Holy See is to designate the next Bishop of the diocese, it seems that he too should assume the office without delay. Moreover, the Holy See may also intend by this appointment to forestall a long vacancy in the diocese because of special circumstances existing therein.

As for the *Auxiliaris,* his office would end with the death of the residential Bishop, unless the apostolic letter of appointment stated otherwise.[59] Accordingly, unless special circumstances make it imperative for the Auxiliary to take office while the principal Bishop is dying, he should not do so, but should wait until the Holy See is consulted. However, if the apostolic letter of appointment states that his office does not cease with that of the principal Bishop, it is certain that the Holy See intends that he continue in office even after the death of the Bishop. He may therefore take possession of his office by presenting the apostolic letter to the Cathedral Chapter or to the diocesan consultors.

Another similar question which is not discussed by authors in

---

[58] Augustine, *loc. cit.*

[59] Can. 355, § 2.

their treatment of Coadjutor Bishops is: What is to be done if the residential Bishop of a diocese dies after the Coadjutor has received the letter of appointment from the Holy See, but before he has taken possession of the office? Here again it is necessary to distinguish. The *Coadiutor datus Sedi* may proceed to the possession of his office for the reason advanced in the preceding paragraph, namely, that his office exists independently of that of the residential Bishop. But it would be a contradiction in terms to speak of a *Coadiutor datus personae Episcopi,* whether he be an *Auxiliaris* or one with the right of succession, assuming office when there is no residential Bishop, for the very notion of these offices demands that there be a residential Bishop in the diocese.

However, since the Holy See in appointing a *Coadiutor cum iure successionis* is also designating the next Bishop of the diocese, it seems unnecessary in this instance to bring the matter to the attention of the Holy See before acting. He may therefore take possession, not of the office of Coadjutorship, but of the diocese, after the manner of residential Bishops[60] and afterward inform the Holy See.

But such action would not be justified in the case of an *Auxiliaris* unless the document of appointment stated that his office does not end with that of the residential Bishop. If the document gives no such indication, then it seems impossible for him to take possession of the office. His office ends with the death of the residential Bishop. Therefore his office ended before it began, or, in other words it could not even begin. On the other hand, if the document stated that the *Auxiliaris* is to continue in office despite the cessation of the office of the residential Bishop, his office as regards its duration is independent of that of the principal Bishop, and it is to be presumed that the Holy See approves of the act of taking possession of the office on his part even after the death of the Bishop to whom he was assigned.

Contrary to these assertions it could perhaps be argued by some that the Holy See should be informed of the changed situation in every case before any further action of taking office, on the ground that the Holy See usually gives as Coadjutor one

[60] Cf. can. 334, § 3.

whose appointment is requested by the residential Bishop. In answer it should be stated that the viewpoint of the succeeding residential Bishop would be at issue only in the appointment of an *Auxiliaris*. In appointing a *Coadiutor datus Sedi* the Holy See always intends that he shall continue in office after the succeeding Bishop assumes the rule of the diocese. The *Coadiutor cum iure successionis* will himself be the succeeding Bishop. When an *Auxiliaris* is to continue in office after the office of the principal Bishop ends, the Holy See intends that this be so regardless of the wishes of the succeeding Bishop. Hence, only when apostolic letter of the appointment of an *Auxiliaris* makes no mention of such continuation in office may it be said that the wishes of the succeeding Bishop are to be considered, and that the Holy See should accordingly be consulted.

CHAPTER VI

POWERS, RIGHTS, AND DUTIES OF COADJUTORS AND AUXILIARIES OF BISHOPS

It is to be expected that among the three types of Coadjutor Bishops there should be many aspects in which they are identical or similar, and many others in which they completely differ. This is especially true of the powers, rights, and duties connected with each Coadjutorship. To avoid repetition and for the sake of clearness and simplicity of treatment, it is best to consider first those powers, rights and duties which are common to all Coadjutors, and then to examine those which are peculiar to one or the other type of Coadjutorship.

It will be possible to consider the powers, rights and duties of a *Coadiutor datus Sedi* under a separate article of this chapter. However, the two types of *Coadiutor datus personae Episcopi*, with and without the right of succession, cannot be treated separately, for the differences in their powers, rights and duties do not depend on the question of the right of succession. The distinction rests rather on the question of whether the principal Bishop is able to direct the affairs of the diocese or whether he is completely incapacitated, regardless of the Coadjutor's status as an *Auxiliaris* or as one who has the right of succession.[1]

ARTICLE 1. POWERS, RIGHTS, AND DUTIES COMMON TO ALL COADJUTORS

Canon 351, § 1: Iura Coadiutoris dati personae Episcopi desumantur ex litteris apostolicis, quibus constituitur.

Canon 352: Coadiutor sedi datus . . . aliis in rebus tantum potest, quantum eidem a Sancta Sede vel ab Episcopo fuerit commissum.

[1] Can. 351, § 2.

The specific powers, rights and duties of the three types of episcopal Coadjutors are indicated briefly in canons 351, 352, and 354 of the Code. The first of these canons refers in part to the *Coadiutor datus personae,* in part also to Coadjutors in general.[2] The second states the powers of the *Coadiutor datus Sedi.* The last treats of the obligation of residence for all Coadjutors. However, these canons for the most part give only general indeterminate rules, leaving much to be specified in the apostolic letter of appointment and within the discretion of the principal Bishop.

In deciding what these powers, rights and duties are in an individual case, one must look first of all to the apostolic letter of appointment.[3] Secondly, the prescriptions of the aforementioned canons are to be considered. Finally, the residential Bishop can add to these powers, rights and duties.[4] The apostolic letter must be acknowledged as holding precedence to any other consideration, even though its specifications appear to indicate rulings contrary to the general norms of the Code. The residential Bishop is not authorized for anything that contradicts the apostolic letter in any way. Hence, all statements in the succeeding articles of this chapter will be subject to the condition that the apostolic letter does not state otherwise.

The office of Coadjutorship as such does not bring with it any ordinary power of jurisdiction,[5] and only the *Coadiutor datus*

---

[2] Contrary to this statement it could be argued that all paragraphs of canon 351 refer exclusively to the *Coadiutor datus personae,* and in no way to the *Coadiutor datus Sedi.* The basis for this claim would be the context of the canon. The first two paragraphs certainly refer exclusively to the *Coadiutor datus personae.* Therefore it could seem that § 3 and § 4 are to be understood in the same sense. However, it is the opinion of the writer that the third and fourth paragraphs do not exclude consideration of the *Coadiutor datus Sedi.* The legislator is careful in § 1 and § 2 of the canon to specify the *Coadiutor datus personae,* whereas in § 3 and § 4 he simply uses the general term *Coadiutor.* It seems therefore safe to presume that § 3 and § 4 include consideration of all Coadjutors. Moreover, regarding the argument from the context, paragraphs § 3 and § 4 are immediately followed by canon 352 which treats exclusively of the *Coadiutor datus Sedi.*

[3] Cans. 351, § 1, and 352.

[4] Cans. 351, § 2, and 352.

[5] Cf. cans. 197 and 198.

Sedi has any ordinary power of orders.[6] Even this latter power is limited, being exclusive of the ordinary power to ordain.[7] Since no Coadjutor has ordinary power of jurisdiction in a diocese, he cannot make use of Canon 81 unless he is given such power by being appointed as Vicar General.[8] Canon 81 provides in part that in emergencies Ordinaries may dispense even from general laws of the Church if the Holy See customarily grants the dispensation and there is grave danger in delay and also difficulty of having recourse to the Holy See. Canon 329, § 1, treating in general of Bishops, says that they have ordinary power,[9] but this statement obviously can be referred only to residential Bishops.[10]

Since ordinary power is seldom granted in the apostolic letter of appointment of Coadjutors, it follows that whatever power they have will for the most part be given by the residential Bishop. Hence, the ruling of Canon 351, § 4:

Canon 351, § 4: Coadiutor, iusto impedimento non detentus, debet, quoties fuerit a Coadiuto requisitus, pontificalia et alias functiones obire, ad quas Episcopus ipse teneretur.

As this rule implies, the residential Bishop should not command the Coadjutor to perform any task which the latter is physically or morally unable to execute. It may happen that the residential Bishop and the Coadjutor will disagree on whether the latter should or should not be assigned a certain work. The Coadjutor may be unwilling to do what is asked of him for the simple reason that he considers his other duties to be as much as he can well perform. When such disagreements arise, it seems that the opinion of the principal Bishop should prevail, for in case of doubt he rather than the Coadjutor should decide whether the Coadjutor can properly do what is required. However, the Coadjutor who feels that he has a just grievance may have recourse to the Holy See.[11]

---

[6] Can. 352.

[7] Can. 352.

[8] Cf. can. 366, § 1.

[9] "Episcopi . . . cum potestate ordinaria regunt sub auctoritate Romani Pontificis."

[10] Cf. can. 334, § 1: "Episcopi residentiales sunt ordinarii . . . pastores. . . ."

[11] Smith, *Elements of Ecclesiastical Law,* I, n. 616.

The Coadjutor must obey the just commands of the Bishop whenever he is requested to perform pontifical or other functions which would otherwise be the duty of the residential Bishop. There are certain limitations, however, in the exercise of pontifical functions by Coadjutor Bishops. For example, in reply to a series of questions the Sacred Congregation of Rites in 1919 ruled that the crozier, since it is a sign of ordinary episcopal jurisdiction, can be used only with the permission of the residential Bishop, and the upper part, or crook, of the crozier is to be turned away from the Coadjutor as he holds it.[12] When the rubrics call for the use of the crozier in a function which the Coadjutor is authorized to perform permission to use it may be presumed. This response refers to a Bishop from an outside diocese, but it seems to apply equally to a Coadjutor Bishop when he pontificates in the diocese wherein he holds his assignment or in another diocese. The Congregation of Rites also ruled that the Coadjutor Bishop who is a Vicar General can bless the people anywhere in the diocese in the manner of the residential Bishop.[13] On this point Augustine,[14] without distinguishing between the Coadjutor who is a Vicar General and one who is not, correctly states that any Coadjutor may bless the people, in or outside of Church, throughout the diocese.[15]

Although canon 337, § 3, states that the residential Bishop may allow another Bishop to use the throne at pontifical functions, he may not grant this permission to his own Coadjutor. This rule was made by the Sacred Congregation of Rites in 1899[16] and reaffirmed by the same Congregation in 1919.[17]

---

[12] S.R.C., *Dubia*, 26 nov. 1919—*AAS*, XII (1920), 178 and 181, ad III, 3; Bouscaren, *The Canon Law Digest*, I, 206.

[13] *AAS*, XII (1920), 180 and 182, ad V, 2; Bouscaren, *The Canon Law Digest*, I, 208.

[14] *A Commentary on the New Code of Canon Law*, II, 381.

[15] Cf. can. 349, § 1, 1°, in relation to can. 239, § 1, 12°.

[16] "An Episcopus Dioecesanus gaudeat iure cedendi Thronum suum alteri Episcopo cum Reverendissimorum Canonicorum adsistentia sibi debita? . . . Affirmative; dummodo Episcopus invitatus non sit ipsius Dioecesani Coadiutor, aut Auxiliaris, aut Vicarius Generalis, aut etiam Dignitas seu Canonicus in illius Ecclesiis. . . ."—S.R.C., decr., 9 maii 1899— *Decr. Auth.*, n. 4023.

[17] *AAS*, XII (1920), 180 and 182, ad V, 3; Bouscaren, *The Canon Law Digest*, I, 208; *Decr. Auth.*, n. 4355.

If the Coadjutor wishes to perform pontifical functions outside of the diocese of his assignment, he needs the permission of his own Bishop to leave the diocese,[18] and also the permission of the Bishop of the other diocese to perform the pontifical functions there.[19] The reasonably presumed permission of the latter Bishop will suffice.[20] If the Coadjutor wishes to pontificate in the church of an exempt clerical community he needs at least the presumed permission of the religious Superior.[21] It does not seem that he need ask his proper Ordinary for permission to pontificate outside his diocese.

Canon 351, § 4, states that the Coadjutor when requested must perform not only the pontifical but also the other functions as well which the residential Bishop would be bound to perform. What is meant here by "other functions"? Chelodi (1880-1922)[22] stated simply that the Coadjutor as far as possible must fulfill the obligations of the resident Bishop as often as he is requested to do so. Wernz[23] and Vidal[24] contended that the *Missa pro populo* was not included. It is true that the celebration of the *Missa pro populo* is primarily the obligation of the residential Bishop, and he should fulfill this obligation personally unless he be unavoidably prevented from doing so.[25] If he is unable to do so on one

[18] Can. 354.

[19] Wernz, *Ius Decretalium,* II, n. 808 (III, a); Wernz-Vidal, *Ius Canonicum,* II, n. 619 (A).

[20] Can. 337, § 1.

[21] Can. 337, § 1.

[22] *Ius de Personis,* n. 196. At first glance it may seem that the words *alias functiones* refer only to non-pontifical ceremonial functions. Canon 462 mentions functions which are reserved to the pastor, and these are almost all ceremonial functions. However, there is one exception. Canon 462, 4° reserves to the pastor the announcement of forthcoming ordinations and marriages. Such announcements cannot be said to be ceremonial in character, and they may at times be posted in a public place according to canons 998, § 1, and 1025. Hence it is justifiable to conclude that the words *alias functiones* of canon 351, § 4, do not refer merely to non-pontifical ceremonial functions, but that Chelodi is correct in assuming that the word *functiones* refers to all obligations of the residential Bishop. Cf. also can. 477, 2.

[23] *Ius Decretalium,* II, n. 808 (III, c).

[24] Wernz-Vidal, *Ius Canonicum,* II, n. 619 (B).

[25] Can. 339, § 4.

of the appointed days,[26] the legislator prefers that the Mass be celebrated by someone else on that day rather than that it should be postponed.[27] If he is unable to do so himself or to have it celebrated by another priest on the day appointed, it should be done as soon as possible thereafter either by the residential Bishop or by some other priest.[28] The wording of canon 351, § 4, seems to indicate that if the residential Bishop cannot say the *Missa pro populo* on the appointed day, he may request the Coadjutor to do so, and then the Coadjutor is bound to comply. If both are prevented on that day, then the Coadjutor has the obligation if he can fulfill it sooner than the residential Bishop. The Coadjutor Bishop is not obliged to offer the *Missa pro populo* for those living in his titular diocese, but the Code recommends that he do this at least from time to time.[29]

It is to be noted that canon 351, § 4, mentions only that the Coadjutor must perform acts which are the duty of the residential Bishop. The Coadjutor should not be required to do anything which does not in any way pertain to the residential Bishop's office.[30]

Once the Coadjutor Bishop has received faculties to act from any lawful authority, whether it be through the apostolic letter of appointment, the Code or the mandate of the residential Bishop, his acts are both licit and valid, and the residential Bishop cannot repeal the acts which the Coadjutor has lawfully performed.[31] Moreover the Coadjutor cannot be punished for so doing, since he has acted within the scope of his authority.[32] But if he has exceeded his authority his act is invalid.[33] The Coadjutor who

[26] Cf. can. 339, § 1.

[27] Can. 339, § 4.

[28] Can. 339, § 4.

[29] Can. 348, § 1.

[30] Toso, *Ad Codicem Iuris Canonici Commentaria Minora* (5 vols., Romae: Marietti, 1920-1927), III, 183: "Excipiendae . . . sunt, ex voluntate expressa Legislatoris, eae functiones, ad quas Episcopus ipse non teneretur; uni namque Episcopo, non aliis, auxilium suum Coadiutor praestare debet." Hereinafter this will be cited *Commentaria Minora.*

[31] Augustine, *A Commentary on the Code of Canon Law,* II, 381; Wernz, *Ius Decretalium,* II, n. 810; Wernz-Vidal, *Ius Canonicum,* II, n. 619 (B).

[32] Augustine, *loc. cit.;* Wernz, *loc. cit.*

[33] Can. 203, § 1.

has done so wilfully may be punished by the principal Bishop in proportion to the gravity of the guilt.[34]

If a Coadjutor should be brought to trial for any delict, the right to judge the case is reserved to the Pope since this is a criminal trial.[35] Canon 1557, § 2, which reserves the conduct of certain trials to the proper tribunals of the Holy See mentions only residential Bishops in the matter of contentious trials. It therefore follows that a Coadjutor who is a defendant in such trials will be judged according to the same rules and by the same tribunals as any other cleric.

The residential Bishop can for a just cause revoke, even totally, faculties which he himself has delegated to the Coadjutor.[36] But faculties of a Coadjutor which derive from the common law or the apostolic letter of appointment cannot be revoked by the principal Bishop, for such action would be a contradiction of the law of a superior. It seems evident, however, that if the use of these faculties conflicts with the certain right of the residential Bishop, the Coadjutor should yield to the wishes of his superior. For example, if the residential Bishop wishes to perform an act for which the Coadjutor has the necessary faculties, or if the residential Bishop wishes to allow another Bishop to do so in one or a few instances, the use of the Coadjutor's faculties may be denied on such occasions.[37]

It has been stated above that the Coadjutor must obey all the just commands of the residential Bishop. This of course includes the acceptance of the faculties delegated by the residential Bishop. Canon 351, § 3, tells in a general way what faculties a residential Bishop should delegate to his Coadjutor rather than to anyone else:

Canon 351, § 3: Quae Coadiutor potest et vult exercere, Episcopus habitualiter alii ne deleget.

At the outset the word *habitualiter* in this law should be emphasized. As stated in the preceding paragraph, there is nothing

[34] Can. 2404.

[35] Cans. 1552, § 2, 2° and 1557, § 1, 3°.

[36] Can. 207, § 1.

[37] Wernz, *Ius Decretalium,* II, n. 808 (IV) and n. 810; Wernz-Vidal, *Ius Canonicum,* II, n. 619 (B); Coronata, *Institutiones Iuris Canonici,* I, n. 408.

to prevent the residential Bishop from delegating authority to someone other than the Coadjutor by way of exception. But when there is occasion for the residential Bishop to delegate some special power to be used constantly by the one delegated, the Coadjutor should be the one chosen unless circumstances dictate the contrary. If the Coadjutor is willing and able to act for the principal Bishop, the delegation should be given to no other. The residential Bishop should presume that the Coadjutor can and is willing to perform the work unless the contrary is evident.[38]

Implied in the above quoted canon is the question of the employment of the Coadjutor as representative or proxy of the residential Bishop. Canons 282, § 1, 286, § 1, 292 and 342 mention instances in which the Coadjutor may be the proxy for the residential Bishop. In view of canon 351, § 3, it appears that the Coadjutor not only may, but has the right, other things being equal, to be appointed the proxy for the residential Bishop.

Canon 282, § 1, includes residential Bishops among those who must attend Plenary Councils, and states that they will have the right to a deliberative, i.e., a deciding, vote in its resolutions. The same canon in paragraph one makes it clear that if the residential Bishop does not attend but wishes to be represented, then his Coadjutor, if he has one, is to be his representative. According to paragraph two of the same canon all titular Bishops must attend if they have been summoned by the Apostolic Legate, and they are presumed to have a deliberative vote unless the letter of convocation states otherwise. But if the residential Bishop is unable to attend, and is represented by his Coadjutor, the latter is entitled to cast not two votes but only one.[39]

As for the role of the Coadjutor at the Provincial Council, he may be invited by the one who will preside, but the consent of a majority of those having a deliberative vote is necessary.[40] If Coadjutor Bishops are convoked to a Provincial Council, the rule for their right to vote is the same as at a Plenary Council, namely that they have a deliberative vote unless the notice of con-

---

[38] Blat, *Commentarium,* II, 322.
[39] Can. 287, § 2.
[40] Can. 286, § 2.

vocation states the contrary. If the Coadjutor is sent as the representative of the principal Bishop, he will likewise have the right to a deliberative vote. There would be no reason for the clause about Coadjutors and Auxiliaries of Bishops in canon 282, § 1, if they do not have a deliberative vote as proxy. For it is evident from canon 287, § 2, that any proxy has at least a consultative vote. Therefore it is to be concluded that canon 282, § 1, is an exception to the general rule of canon 287, § 2.

In the interval between the Provincial Councils, the Metropolitan is to call a meeting of his suffragans at least every five years.[41] At these meetings problems of the various dioceses in the Province are discussed, and plans are made for the next Provincial Council. Coadjutor Bishops are to be called to these meetings[42] and if the residential Bishop cannot attend, the Coadjutor should be his representative.[43]

The Coadjutor is not listed in the Code among those who must be notified to attend the diocesan synod,[44] nor among those who may but need not be notified for attendance.[45] From the wording of canon 358, § 1, it cannot be claimed that the Coadjutor Bishop must be notified to attend the synod unless he is the Vicar General or a vicar forane, or holds one of the other positions mentioned therein. The second paragraph of this canon, however, allows the residential Bishop to summon other priests as well when they can attend without prejudice to the parochial care of souls. It would certainly be inappropriate if without a just cause the Coadjutor were not asked to be present. When invited to the synod, the Coadjutor has the right to vote unless the residential Bishop should decree otherwise in the letter of invitation.[46]

The Coadjutor Bishop may also be sent as representative of the residential Bishop in making the so called *ad limina* visit to the tombs of Saints Peter and Paul and to the Holy Father every

---

[41] Can. 292, § 1.

[42] Can. 292, § 2.

[43] Coronata, *Institutiones Iuris Canonici*, I, n. 405 (4°); Sipos, *Enchiridion*, n. 51 (5).

[44] Can. 358, § 1.

[45] Can. 358, § 2.

[46] Can. 358, § 2.

five or ten years.[47] The residential Bishop may send the Coadjutor in his place if circumstances so demand, but he may send some priest to represent him on this visit only with the previous approval of the Holy See.[48] Ordinarily the Coadjutor is obliged to make the *ad limina* visit only if he is sent by the principal Bishop, and not in virtue of his own office.[49] Canon 341, § 1, implies this, since it rules that Bishops are to make the visit in the same year in which they are to sęnd a report to the Holy See on the state of their respective dioceses. Only the *Coadiutor datus personae inhabili* makes this report. Hence only such a coadjutor has the obligation of the *ad limina* visit.

The canons cited above mention occasions on which the Coadjutor Bishop, rather than anyone else, should represent the principal Bishop. These are, however, but a few of the possible instances in which the Coadjutor should be chosen to act for the Bishop to whom he is assigned. It may be said that according to canon 351, § 3, the Coadjutor, unless there is good reason for the contrary, should be chosen to represent the residential Bishop on all occasions when the residential Bishop, if he acted himself, would act in his capacity as the ruling Bishop of the diocese.

It frequently happens that the Coadjutor Bishop of a diocese is also its Vicar General.[50] Coronata[51] maintains that there is never an obligation on the part of the residential Bishop to appoint the Coadjutor as his Vicar General. It is not the intention of the writer to contend that the Coadjutor should always be chosen for this position. But, unless there is some compelling reason why it should not be done, it seems that the Coadjutor Bishop should be appointed Vicar General in preference to any other priest of the diocese.

The Coadjutor Bishop, having been honored by the Church with promotion to the episcopacy, is second only to the residen-

---

[47] Cans. 342 and 341, § 1.

[48] Can. 342.

[49] Wernz, *Ius Decretalium,* II, n. 808 (III, c) ; Smith, *Elements of Ecclesiastical Law,* I, n. 613.

[50] Beste, *Introductio in Codicem,* p. 273; De Meester, *Compendium,* II, n. 704.

[51] *Institutiones Iuris Canonici,* I, n. 405 (footnote).

tial Bishop in dignity within the diocese. It is only fitting that this honor should be reflected also, as far as possible, in the matter of jurisdiction. Here too the Coadjutor should be second only to the Bishop. It does not seem congruous that he who is superior in the power of orders should be inferior in the power of jurisdiction. And this appears to be the mind of the legislator. For, canon 351, § 3, states that the residential Bishop should not delegate to a third party what the Coadjutor can and is willing to perform. It is true that in appointing a Vicar General there is question, not of delegated power, but of the conferring of ordinary power of jurisdiction. But canon 351, § 3, equivalently makes the Coadjutor Bishop the *alter ego* of the principal Bishop whenever there is any power to be delegated habitually. The Vicar General is intended to be the *alter ego* of the principal Bishop in matters of jurisdiction. From what has already been said about the Coadjutor as the representative of the residential Bishop at Plenary or Provincial Councils and for the *ad limina* visit, it is evident that the legislator prefers that the Coadjutor act for the residential Bishop whenever a representative is needed and it is possible for the Coadjutor to act in this capacity. No mention of the Vicar General is made in those canons.

In treating of the Vicar General's right of precedence[52] the Code implies that a Coadjutor Bishop is not necessarily the Vicar General in the diocese, for it rules that the Vicar General precedes every cleric who is not a Bishop. This does not contradict the claim made in the preceding paragraph. There may be times when it would be imprudent for the residential Bishop to add the duties of a Vicar General to those the Coadjutor already has. As Chelodi points out,[53] the *Coadiutor datus Sedi* is usually given by the Holy See because of the large size of the diocese for the purpose of exercising the episcopal power of orders. And so the residential Bishop would seldom give him power of jurisdiction. The same would hold true for any Coadjutor whose other duties make it inadvisable that he have added to them the duties implied in the additional power of jurisdiction. Ultimately it is the right of the

[52] Can. 370, § 1.

[53] *Ius de Personis,* n. 196.

principal Bishop to decide whether the Coadjutor is capable of properly fulfilling the office of Vicar General in addition to his other duties.

When the residential Bishop is absent from the diocese, it is the Vicar General who should rule the diocese in his place,[54] and this is an additional reason why it is more appropriate that the Coadjutor Bishop be the Vicar General. In the residential Bishop's absence the Coadjutor can at least be given delegated power equal in extent to the ordinary power of the Vicar General. Instead, it often happens in the United States that the chancellor is appointed to act for the Bishop in his absence or when he cannot perform certain matters of jurisdiction in person. Prince[55] justly complains that the practice in this country of habitually delegating to the chancellor powers which belong to the Vicar General tends to relegate the latter's office to a merely honorary position. It is his contention that such habitual delegation of power cannot be defended, though the occasional delegation of power to the chancellor is often warranted.[56] Inasmuch as the special jurisdiction in which chancellors share is simply a delegated power, the practice of thus habitually delegating them in dioceses which have a Coadjutor Bishop is completely in opposition to canon 351, § 3, if the Coadjutor is able and willing to do what has been delegated to the chancellor. The chancellor has the duties of keeping the diocesan archives in order and of acting as curial notary.[57] It is of course evident that these functions should not be assigned to the Coadjutor.

From the time that the Coadjutor takes possession of his office he has the right to an income from some diocesan source.[58] It is primarily the duty of the residential Bishop to provide for his support.[59] The apostolic letter of appointment may give some di-

---

[54] Cf. can. 368, § 1.

[55] *The Diocesan Chancellor,* The Catholic University of America Canon Law Studies, n. 167 (Washington, D. C.: The Catholic University of America Press, 1942), p. 95.

[56] Prince, *op. cit.,* p. 101.

[57] Can. 372.

[58] Wernz-Vidal, *Ius Canonicum,* II, n. 619 (B, b).

[59] Wernz-Vidal, *loc. cit.;* Wernz, *Ius Decretalium,* II, n. 808 (III, d).

rections in this matter,[60] and if so these are to be observed. At times the apostolic letter may allow the Coadjutor to retain some benefice or other incumbency which provided for him a source of income previously to his designation as Coadjutor.[61]

Concerning the obligation of Coadjutors to reside within the diocese to which they are appointed, the rule is as follows:

Canon 354: Coadiutor quilibet obligatione tenetur, sicut Episcopus, residendi in dioecesi, e qua, extra tempus vacationum, ad normam can. 338, ipsi non licet, nisi ad breve tempus, Coadiuto permittente, discedere.

Since this canon refers to canon 338 in a general way, and not to any particular paragraph or paragraphs, it may be concluded that all the parts of that canon apply equally to Coadjutors and residential Bishops. Canon 338 rules that the residential Bishop is himself held to the law of residence notwithstanding the fact that he has a Coadjutor. The time spent in making the *ad limina* visit, in attending Councils, or in the performance of any duties of office which necessitate an absence from the diocese is not to be included as part of the vacation allowed to residential Bishops or Coadjutors. Apart from such causes the maximum allowed absence from the diocese is three months, whether continuous or interrupted. This time of vacation may not be made one with the time of absence allowed in connection with promotion to the Episcopate, with the *ad limina* visit, or with attendance at Councils. Neither may the time of vacation be connected continuously with that of the following year.[62] Unless a grave and urgent cause excuses, the Coadjutor is bound, as is the residential Bishop, to be present in his diocese during Advent and Lent, and for the feasts of Christmas, Easter, Pentecost and Corpus Christi.[63] The Coadjutor's absence from the diocese of his assignment beyond six months is to be brought to the attention of the Holy See by the Metropolitan.[64]

---

[60] Coronata, *Institutiones Iuris Canonici,* I, n. 406 (6) ; Smith, *Elements of Ecclesiastical Law,* I, 616; Wernz-Vidal, *loc. cit.*

[61] Sipos, *Enchiridion,* n. 51.

[62] Can. 338, § 2.

[63] Can. 338, § 3.

[64] Can. 338, § 4.

The time and length of the Coadjutor's vacation is to be determined by the residential Bishop or with his approval. Outside of the vacation period the Coadjutor may leave the diocese for only a short time, generally taken to mean no more than seven days,[65] and then only with the permission of the residential Bishop. Smith,[66] writing before the promulgation of the Code, asserted that whenever possible the Coadjutor should live in the residence of the principal Bishop. However, this obligation is in no way indicated in the Code of Canon Law.

Apart from the powers, rights and duties already mentioned, there are others which Coadjutors have in common with residential Bishops. They have of course the privileges enumerated in canon 349, § 1, which are common to both residential and titular Bishops. Some of these have been treated in the preceding paragraphs of this article. The privileges of even titular Bishops are effective from the time they are notified of their deputation as Coadjutors, and not merely after they have taken canonical possession of their office.[67]

In common with Cardinals and other Bishops, Coadjutors have the privilege of using the portable altar everywhere, even at sea with the proper precautions, and of following their own *ordo* wherever they say Mass.[68] When they celebrate Mass they have the benefit of the personally privileged altar.[69] Provided that they have no obligation of celebrating Mass in the Cathedral Church, they may themselves celebrate Mass and also allow another priest to celebrate Mass in their presence anywhere, even with the portable altar. They may also celebrate Mass on Holy Thursday and three Masses on Christmas night, or allow some priest to do so in their presence.[70]

Together with members of their household they may gain indulgences in their own chapels for which the visit to a church or

---

[65] Coronata, *Institutiones Iuris Canonici,* I, n. 407.

[66] *Elements of Ecclesiastical Law,* I, n. 616.

[67] Can. 349, § 1.

[68] Cans. 349, § 1, 1° and 239, § 1, nn. 7°, 8°, 9°.

[69] Cans. 349, § 1, 1°, and 239, § 1, n. 10°.

[70] Cans. 349, § 1, and 239, § 1, nn. 4° and 7°.

shrine is prescribed.[71] The Coadjutor may also choose for himself and his household a priest for the hearing of confessions, and this priest, if he be without confessional jurisdiction, automatically obtains faculties to absolve them even from all reserved sins and censures with the exception of censures *specialissimo modo* reserved to the Holy See and the censures resulting from the revelation of a secret of the Holy Office.[72] Coadjutors need only the presumed permission of the Ordinary to preach in any diocese.[73] Finally, Coadjutors have the same rights as Cardinals in blessing sacred objects and attaching to them the indulgences granted by the Holy See, as well as the right to erect the Way of the Cross. In doing so, however, they must observe all the rites prescribed in the rubrics.[74]

Such are the powers, rights and duties common to all Coadjutor Bishops. There are of course many others implied in the very nature of their office. Coadjutors are given to aid the residential Bishop as much as is in their power. In general, they should, just as the residential Bishop, beware of any dangers to the faith and morals of the people within their dioceses, and make prudent recommendations to the principal Bishop.[75]

ARTICLE 2. POWERS, RIGHTS, AND DUTIES OF THE *Coadiutor Datus Personae*

Canon 351, § 2: Nisi aliud in his [apostolicis] litteris caveatur, Coadiutor qui datur Episcopo prorsus inhabili, habet omnia iura ac officia episcopalia; ceteri tantum possunt quantum Episcopus eisdem commiserit.

As heretofore stated, the powers, rights and duties of the *Coadiutor datus personae* have no necessary connection with the fact that he has or has not the right of future succession to the episcopal see. It is possible for an *Auxiliaris* to have even greater

[71] Cans. 349, § 1, 1°, and 239, § 1, n. 11°.
[72] Cans. 349, § 1, 1°, and 239, § 1, n. 2°.
[73] Cans. 349, § 1, 1°, and 239, § 1, n. 3°.
[74] Cans. 349, § 1, 1°, and 239, § 1, nn. 5°-6°.
[75] Cf. can. 336, §2.

powers than a Coadjutor who has the right of future succession. Canon 351, § 2, is proof that the most important factor in determining these powers, rights and duties is the physical and mental condition of the Bishop to whom the Coadjutor is assigned, that is, the fact whether the residential Bishop is, in the words of the Code, *habilis* or *inhabilis*.

Concerning the powers, rights, and duties of the *Coadiutor datus personae habili* there is little to be said beyond what has already been stated in the preceding article. As the above quoted canon 351, § 2, states, he has only as much power as the residential Bishop commits to him. Even though he may have the right of succession, he depends entirely on the residential Bishop for permission to exercise the powers of orders or of jurisdiction, and he must obey all the just commands of the principal Bishop.

Before treating the specific powers, rights and duties of a *Coadiutor datus personae inhabili,* one must ascertain the meaning of the words *prorsus inhabili* as used in canon 351, § 2. The English equivalent of *prorsus inhabili,* as used here, is "*completely incapacitated.*" But whether this incapacity of the residential Bishop is to be understood in the sense of canon 353, § 3,[76] namely that he cannot even place a human act, is not easily decided. It is possible for one to be unable to fulfill any of the duties of an office, and yet be able to place a human act. What constitutes complete incapacity in particular cases is not immediately evident. Wernz[77] and Vidal[78] give only insanity as an example, thus implying that the residential Bishop must be incapable of a human act before the rule of canon 351, § 2, finds application. This appears to be the safest interpretation, for it is well nigh impossible to decide what degree of incapacity, short of the inability to place a human act, would be sufficient to declare the resident Bishop *prorsus inhabilis*. As long as he is able to direct the affairs of his diocese, even from a sick-bed, he is not *inhabilis* in the sense in which it is taken here.

---

[76] "Si Episcopus eum in statum inciderit ut eliciendi actus humani sit impos. . . ."

[77] *Ius Decretalium,* II, n. 810.

[78] Wernz-Vidal, *Ius Canonicum,* II, n. 619 (B).

Since it may be difficult to decide whether the degree of incapacity of the principal Bishop is sufficient for the application of the rule, the apostolic letter of appointment should either state that the residential Bishop is to be considered as incapacitated, or else indicate clearly what powers, rights and duties belong to the Coadjutor. If the apostolic letter is silent on these points, it should be presumed that the residential Bishop is *habilis*. This presumption may be overruled if it has become evident that, due to insanity or weakness, the principal Bishop cannot properly administer the rule of the diocese. But in doubtful cases it is best that the matter be brought to the attention of the Holy See.

The wording of canon 351, § 2, gives rise to a difficulty which may be formulated as follows: Does its rule apply only in instances wherein the residential Bishop is incapacitated before the Coadjutor has received his appointment, or does it apply equally if the residential Bishop becomes unable to fulfill his duties some time after the Coadjutor's reception of the apostolic letter of appointment or after he has taken canonical possession of his office? Or again, does the rule apply if the principal Bishop's total incapacitation is only temporary?

The Code does not distinguish between these various situations. On the one hand, canon 351, § 2, may be understood to refer only to a residential Bishop who is permanently incapacitated at the time the Coadjutor is assigned to the diocese. If after the Coadjutor's appointment the residential Bishop is disabled, the Vicar General should act in his place. On the other hand, it does not seem that the wording of canon 351, § 2, contradicts the opinion that a *Coadiutor datus personae habili* automatically becomes a *Coadiutor datus personae inhabili* when the residential Bishop becomes completely incapacitated. Hence, according to this opinion, the *Coadiutor datus personae* should assume complete control of the diocese, not only when the residential Bishop is totally *inhabilis* at the time of the Coadjutor's deputation by the Holy See, but also if at any time thereafter the residential Bishop becomes completely incapacitated, whether the incapacity be temporary or permanent. If the disability of the residential Bishop proves to be only temporary, the power which was assumed by the Coadjutor reverts once more to the residential Bishop.

The difficulty occasioned by these contradictory opinions would be obviated if the Coadjutor Bishop were at the same time the Vicar General, and this furnishes an additional argument in favor of the appointment of the Coadjutor to that position. But if such is not the case, should the Vicar General or the Coadjutor rule the diocese when the residential Bishop is incapacitated? The wording of canon 351, § 2, is not conclusive for either opinion. However, canon 429, § 1, rules that if the residential Bishop is incapacitated or forcibly kept from ruling the diocese, the Vicar General or some other priest appointed by the residential Bishop shall rule in his place. No mention is made of the Coadjutor Bishop. Hence, to say that the Coadjutor should supersede the Vicar General in such circumstances would be to claim an exception to canon 429, § 1. For this reason the safer opinion seems to be that a Coadjutor is to be considered as given to a disabled Bishop in the sense of canon 351, § 2, only when the apostolic letter of appointment indicates that the reason for the appointment is the disability of the residential Bishop. At other times, the incapacity of the residential Bishop is to be supplied by the Vicar General, or by some other priest designated by the Bishop in accordance with canon 429, §1.

It may be asked whether the *Coadjutor datus personae inhabili* should be referred to as an Ordinary in virtue of his status as ruler of the diocese (if one prescind now from the fact that he is or is not the Vicar General). The question is a purely academic one and of little practical import. For if he is not an Ordinary in the strict sense, he is an Ordinary in everything but name, since he has all the rights and duties formerly held by the principal Bishop.

Canon 198, § 1, offers an exhaustive list of those who are properly referred to as Ordinaries. None of the three types of Coadjutors are specifically mentioned, nor can any Coadjutor be understood as included among those who rule the diocese when it is without a residential Bishop.[79] However, according to Wernz-

[79] ". . . Episcopus residentialis . . . itemque ii qui praedictis deficientibus interim ex iuris praescripto aut ex probatis constitutionibus succedunt in regimine. . . ." The difficulty centers about the interpretation of the word

Vidal[80] the term *Ordinarius* is reserved in law for those who have ordinary power of jurisdiction both in the internal and in the external forum. The office of the Coadjutor of a disabled Bishop certainly satisfies this condition. Therefore, despite the aforementioned argument to the contrary, it seems correct to refer to the Coadjutor as an Ordinary. Otherwise, if it happens that the Coadjutor of a disabled Bishop is not the Vicar General of the diocese, it would mean that the latter is an Ordinary whereas his superior, the Coadjutor, is not. Moreover, there may be two or even three Ordinaries in the same diocese.[81]

Canon 351, § 2, states simply that the Coadjutor of a totally incapacitated Bishop has all episcopal rights and duties. He assumes all the power ordinarily held by a residential Bishop, and since he has all episcopal rights and duties his status is equal to that of the residential Bishop. However, he does not receive special personal privileges over and above those of residential Bishops in general (e.g., privileges of Cardinals not had by other Bishops),[82] even though the principal Bishop enjoyed such privileges.

Since canon 351, § 2, gives the *Coadiutor datus personae inhabili* all the rights of the residential Bishop, and since among the rights of the residential Bishop is that of erecting a pontifical throne in any church of the diocese,[83] it would therefore seem that the Coadjutor of a disabled Bishop likewise has this right. But mention has already been made of a decision of the Sacred Congregation of Rites forbidding the residential Bishop to give permission to the Coadjutor to use the throne. There is a difficulty here of deciding which is the rule and which the exception. Does the Coadjutor of a disabled Bishop have all the rights formerly had by the principal Bishop with the exception of the use of the pontifical throne? Or is it correct to say rather that

"*deficientibus.*" Except for the Coadjutor, there is no one present to rule the diocese. On the other hand, the diocese does not lack a residential Bishop even when he is incapacitated.

[80] *Ius Canonicum,* II, n. 367.

[81] Cf. can. 366, § 3.

[82] Cf. cans. 239 and 349.

[83] Can. 349, § 2, 3°.

no Coadjutor may use the pontifical throne except the Coadjutor of a totally disabled Bishop, since this Coadjutor has all episcopal rights?

It may further be asked whether there is a real contradiction between the ruling of canon 351, § 2, and the decision of the Sacred Congregation of Rites. The aforementioned decree of the Sacred Congregation referred to the granting of permission by the principal Bishop for the Coadjutor to use the pontifical throne. In the present instance there is no question of the permission of the residential Bishop, but of a permission implied in the law itself by the general rule of canon 351, § 2. It could thus seem logical to conclude that, although the residential Bishop can never give the Coadjutor permission to use the throne, the Code gives this power to the Coadjutor of a totally disabled Bishop. However, despite this argument, it seems to the writer that, in view of the wording of canon 2, no Coadjutor has the privilege of erecting a pontifical throne in any church of the diocese unless a special indult from the Holy See has been obtained. Canon 2 says in part that all liturgical laws remain in force unless they are *expressly* overruled in the Code. At most, it can only be doubtfully claimed that the right of the *Coadiutor datus personae inhabili* to use the pontifical throne is implied in the Code. In the absence of an express permission the safest course is to interpret strictly the ruling of the Sacred Congregation of Rites as applying to all Coadjutors without exception.

Canon 349, § 2, mentions two other rights of the residential Bishop. There seems to be no reason to doubt that in virtue of canon 351, § 2, these are had by the Coadjutor of a disabled Bishop. One is the right to grant indulgences of one hundred days within the diocesan territory.[84] The other is the right to the revenues provided for the Bishop's table expenses. Whereas the principal Bishop previously had the obligation to support the

---

[84] Cf. can. 349, § 2, 2°. This canon accords to residential Bishops the right to grant indulgences of fifty days, but this number of days has now been increased to one hundred. Cf. S. Poenit. Ap., 20 iul. 1942—*AAS*, XXXIV (1942), 240: Bouscaren, *The Canon Law Digest,* II, 221.

Coadjutor, the latter now has the duty to support in a fitting manner the disabled Bishop.[85]

A question arises with regard to the mention of the Bishop's name in the first prayer of the Canon of the Mass. If a Coadjutor is given full ordinary power in the apostolic letter of appointment, or if he receives such power because of the disability of the residential Bishop, it could by some be argued that, since the Coadjutor has the responsibility and need of prayers in administering the diocese, he should at least be mentioned in the Mass along with the principal Bishop. However, even in such a case only the principal Bishop, and not the Coadjutor with full ordinary power, should be mentioned. The prayer reads *"et Antistite nostro N."* There is only one principal Bishop in any diocese. As long as he continues to be the principal Bishop, he has the exclusive right to be mentioned in this prayer, for he alone holds the episcopal benefice. The Sacred Congregation of Rites replied to this effect in 1882 in reference to the Coadjutor of the Archdiocese of Pisa.[86] Sometimes the apostolic letter directs that the name of the residential Bishop alone be mentioned in the Mass. But even if no mention of this is made, the same practice should be observed in similar situations everywhere.

Since canon 351, § 2, assigns to the Coadjutor of a totally disabled Bishop all the duties of the episcopal office, it seems that the obligation to celebrate the *Missa pro populo* on the designated days likewise devolves on the Coadjutor Bishop. Some authors[87] claim that the *Missa pro populo* is not included among the duties of any Coadjutor, even though the principal Bishop is disabled. The basis for their contention is that canon 475, § 2, in ruling on the rights and duties of a *vicarius adiutor* given to a disabled pastor, states that he has all the duties of the pastor except the

---

[85] Can. 349, § 2, 1°, in conjunction with can. 351, § 2.

[86] S.R.C., *Pisana,* 11 mart. 1882—*Decr. Auth.,* n. 3538.

[87] Cappello, *Tractatus Canonico-Moralis de Sacramentis iuxta Codicem Iuris Canonici* (3 vols. in 6, Taurinorum Angustae: Marietti, 1921-1939), I, n. 368, 2; Wernz-Vidal, *Ius Canonicum,* II, n. 619; Toso, *Commentaria Minora,* III, 183; Donnellan, *The Obligation of the Missa Pro Populo,* The Catholic University of America Canon Law Studies, n. 155 (Washington, D. C.: The Catholic University of America Press, 1942), p. 59.

application of the *Missa pro populo*. Canon 351, § 2, however, states no such exception. Even though the duties of a *vicarius adiutor* are in many respects similar to those of a Coadjutor of a disabled Bishop, it seems fair to conclude that if the legislator intended this exception as in the case of the *vicarius adiutor,* it would have been specifically mentioned. The *vicarius adiutor* has the duty to see to it that the *Missa pro populo* is said if the pastor is unable to see to it himself, but it is not his personal responsibility to offer the Mass.[88] Nevertheless, for the reason already stated, the Coadjutor of a disabled Bishop, unlike the *vicarius adiutor,* assumes the obligation of the *Missa pro populo* in addition to the other duties of the residential Bishop.

Regarding the diocesan synod, Toso[89] holds that no Coadjutor, even though he has the right of succession, may convoke the synod unless this is expressly granted in the letter of his deputation. Donnelly[90] denies that this is true of the Coadjutor given to a disabled Bishop, and claims that he may convoke a synod if he judges it advisable or necessary. Donnelly's opinion seems to be the more tenable, for, as he points out, canon 351, § 2, explicitly grants to a Coadjutor given to a Bishop who is totally incapacitated all the rights of the episcopal office. The synod of course should not be convoked if it is foreseen that the principal Bishop will soon recover from his malady.

A pre-Code author, Smith,[91] stated that the Coadjutor of a disabled Bishop receives all the powers held by the residential Bishop, except that he cannot alienate church property. This limitation is not indicated in the Code. Therefore, if he sees fit to do so, he may alienate ecclesiastical goods within the limits allowed residential Bishops by the Code[92] or by special faculties granted by the Holy See.

---

[88] Bastnagel, "The *Vicarius Adiutor* and the *Missa pro populo*"—*The Jurist,* V (1945), p. 126.

[89] *Commentaria Minora,* III, 188.

[90] *The Diocesan Synod,* The Catholic University of America Canon Law Studies, n. 74 (Washington, D. C.: The Catholic University of America 1932), p. 49.

[91] *Elements of Ecclesiastical Law,* I, n. 616.

[92] Cf. can. 1532.

Besides the powers and rights derived from the common law, the *Coadiutor datus personae inhabili* has also all the rights and powers which were given by delegation of special faculties from the Holy See to the residential Bishop. If the latter had been appointed to execute any papal rescripts, such as the granting of dispensations, indulgences, privileges, or benefices, and had not yet done so before becoming incapacitated, his Coadjutor may take his place in their execution, unless the residential Bishop had been chosen because of exclusive personal qualifications.[93] When the papal rescript refers to the title or office of the residential Bishop, it is to be presumed that he was not chosen because of special fitness for the work.[94]

In general, the *Coadiutor datus personae inhabili,* in exercising his rule of the diocese, should do nothing which might prejudice the rights of his successor (if the Coadjutor is an *Auxiliaris*), or of the principal Bishop, should he recover and resume his administration.

ARTICLE 3. POWERS, RIGHTS, AND DUTIES OF THE *Coadiutor Datus Sedi*

Canon 352: Coadiutor sedi datus potest in territorio ea quae sunt ordinis episcopalis exercere, excepta sacra ordinatione; aliis in rebus tantum potest, quantum eidem a Sancta Sede vel ab Episcopo fuerit commissum.

Canon 352 indicates the essential difference between Coadjutors given to the episcopal see and Coadjutors given to the person of the Bishop. The *Coadiutor datus Sedi* may, whenever he sees fit, exercise the episcopal power of orders with the exception of the ordination of clerics. The *Coadiutor datus personae* does not have this power in virtue of his office, unless the residential Bishop is totally disabled, as explained in the preceding article.

Therefore the *Coadiutor datus Sedi* may on his own authority

---

[93] Can. 58.

[94] O'Neill, *Papal Rescripts of Favor,* The Catholic University of America Canon Law Studies, n. 57 (Washington, D. C.: The Catholic University of America, 1930), p. 186.

confer the Sacrament of Confirmation, consecrate chalices, bless and consecrate churches, and, in a word, do everything for which the episcopal power of orders is necessary, save only the function of ordaining. This power he may exercise without informing or obtaining the permission of the residential Bishop.[95] Ordinarily the residential Bishop has no right to forbid the use of this power, since its source is the law itself, but the Coadjutor should act in accordance with the reasonable requests of the principal Bishop. If they should disagree on matters concerning the exercise of the episcopal power of orders and the Coadjutor is unwilling to accede to the wish of the residential Bishop, the Holy See should be asked to decide the matter. It is evident, however, that this right of the *Coadiutor datus Sedi* must yield to the superior right of the residential Bishop, should the latter wish to exercise the episcopal power of orders on any occasion.[96] Moreover, in accordance with canon 351, § 3, the residential Bishop may also delegate some Bishop other than the *Coadiutor datus Sedi* to perform pontifical functions, but he may not do this habitually.

While the power of exercising episcopal orders possessed by the *Coadiutor datus Sedi* is ordinary power,[97] he is not an Ordinary in virtue of his office. The definition of an Ordinary[98] postulates ordinary power of jurisdiction. Since the common law does not give the *Coadiutor datus Sedi* any power of jurisdiction, he is not an Ordinary. Therefore the *Coadiutor datus Sedi* cannot make use of the emergency powers of canon 81 unless he is also the Vicar General.

The *Coadiutor datus Sedi* is forbidden to ordain clerics within the diocese of his appointment without the permission of the residential Bishop. This restriction extends also to the conferral of the first tonsure.[99] All ordinations are therefore reserved to the

---

[95] De Meester, *Compendium,* II, n. 704 (V) ; Claeys Bouuaert-Simenon, *Manuale Juris Canonici* (3 vols., Vols. I et III, 3 ed., Gandae et Leodii: apud Auctores, 1930-1931), I, n. 493.

[96] Claeys Bouuaert-Simenon, *loc. cit.*

[97] Coronata, *Institutiones Iuris Canonici,* I, n. 406 (2) ; Toso, *Commentaria Minora,* III, 183.

[98] Wernz-Vidal, *Ius Canonicum,* II, 367.

[99] Can. 950.

principal Bishop. However, if the principal Bishop cannot personally attend to all the necessary ordinations within his diocese, he should assign this work to his Coadjutor.[100] The residential Bishop may at times allow another Bishop than his Coadjutor to ordain, but to do so habitually would be contrary to the ruling of canon 351, § 3.

The words *aliis in rebus* of canon 352 refer to matters of jurisdiction and administration.[101] The position of the *Coadiutor datus Sedi* as regards the power of jurisdiction and administration is identical with that of the *Coadiutor datus personae habili,* that is, he depends entirely on the principal Bishop for delegation in these matters, unless the apostolic letter of appointment states otherwise. Chelodi[102] has already been cited to the effect that the *Coadiutor datus Sedi* seldom shares in the jurisdiction and administration of a diocese, inasmuch as the reason for his appointment is usually the necessity of the frequent exercise of the power of episcopal orders. But should it happen that the *Coadiutor datus Sedi* can properly fulfill the work of jurisdiction or administration in addition to his other duties, these should not be habitually delegated to anyone else.[103]

If the residential Bishop becomes incapacitated at any time, either before or after the taking of canonical possession of office by the *Coadiutor datus Sedi,* the latter does not assume the disabled Bishop's powers and duties. The powers, rights, and duties of the *Coadiutor datus Sedi* are not affected by the disability of the principal Bishop, but rather remain the same as before.

---

[100] Coronata, *loc. cit.*

[101] Beste, *Introductio in Codicem,* p. 273.

[102] *Ius de Personis,* n. 196.

[103] Can. 351, § 3.

CHAPTER VII

Expiration of the Office of Coadjutor Bishops

Canon 355, § 1. Coadiutor cum iure successionis, vacante sede episcopali, statim evadit Ordinarius dioecesis, pro qua fuerat constitutus, dummodo possessionem legitime ceperit, ad normam can. 353.

§ 2. Cum Episcopi munere exspirat Auxiliaris officium, nisi aliud in litteris apostolicis caveatur.

§ 3. Si Coadiutor datus fuerit sedi, eius officium etiam sede vacante perdurat.

As the canon here quoted shows, the effect of the residential Bishop's cessation from office on the status of Coadjutor Bishops differs for each type of Coadjutorship. It should first of all be noted that the office of the principal Bishop must truly have ceased before the rules of canon 355 take effect. This would not be so if the principal Bishop were exiled, forcibly expelled from his diocese, or in any way prevented from exercising the rule of the diocese.[1] The office of the residential Bishop may expire not only through his death, but also through his resignation, deprivation, or removal from office, or in consequence of his transfer to another diocese.[2] Only in such cases does canon 355 find application.

When the office of the Bishop to whom he was assigned expires, the Coadjutor with the right of succession ceases to be a Coadjutor and automatically becomes the principal Bishop of the diocese. No other act, such as the taking of possession, is necessary on his part.[3] Canon 355, § 1, adds the condition that such a Coadjutor must have taken canonical possession of his office as Coadjutor in accordance with canon 353. The fulfillment of this condition is necessary for the validity of the Coadjutor's succession, since

[1] Cf. can. 429.

[2] Can. 183, § 1.

[3] Coronata, *Institutiones Iuris Canonici*, I, n. 408; Wernz-Vidal, *Ius* Canonicum, II, n. 618.

the word *dummodo* is used.[4] However, even if the Coadjutor has failed or has been unable to take possession of his office, he may nevertheless present the apostolic letter of his appointment as Coadjutor to the Chapter or diocesan consultors after the expiration of the office of the principal Bishop.[5] Thereupon he immediately becomes the principal Bishop of the diocese. But while this would usually be the case, it seems doubtful that the Coadjutor with the right of succession may thus become the principal Bishop unless he has received the episcopal consecration within three months and has taken canonical possession of his Coadjutorship within four months after the reception of the document of appointment, or was inculpably prevented from doing so.[6] Failing in this the Coadjutor would forfeit his right to the Coadjutorship, and hence also the right to succeed to the rule of the diocese. In such an eventuality all the pertinent facts should be reported as soon as possible to the Holy See, which will then decide whether to reaffirm the Coadjutor's right of succession, or to appoint another in his place.

The office of the *Auxiliaris* ceases simultaneously with that of the Bishop to whom he was assigned, unless the apostolic letter of deputation states otherwise. If the apostolic letter says nothing about this, a document of reappointment of the *Auxiliaris* by the Holy See is necessary when the succeeding Bishop is assigned to the diocese. Wernz,[7] treating of the *Coadiutor temporalis* (a term equivalent to the present *Auxiliaris*), claimed that the recovery of a residential Bishop who had been incapacitated causes the office of his *Coadiutor temporalis* to cease. This view is not presented in any of the commentaries written since the promulgation of the Code. Nor is it in any way implied in canon 355, § 2, which states merely that the office of the Coadjutor without the right of succession ends with that of the residential Bishop.

DeMeester[8] holds that the office of *Auxiliaris* is revocable at the will of the Roman Pontiff, but not so the office of *Coadiutor cum*

[4] Can. 39; Coronata, *loc. cit.*

[5] Coronata, *loc. cit.;* Beste, *Introductio in Codicem,* p. 273.

[6] Can. 333.

[7] *Ius Decretalium,* II, n. 810 (IV).

[8] *Compendium,* II, n. 704 (VII).

iure successionis. The latter, he maintains, can be recalled only for the usual canonical reasons, since by his appointment he has acquired a *ius ad rem* to the office and benefice of the residential Bishop.

The duration of the office of the *Coadiutor datus Sedi,* unlike the other types of Coadjutorship, is not affected by the cessation of the office by the principal Bishop. His office continues, as before, during the vacancy of the see, but he is then subject to the Chapter or the Vicar Capitular who rules the diocese at that time,[9] unless the contrary is stated in the apostolic letter of appointment.[10]

On becoming the principal Bishop, the Coadjutor with the right of succession immediately loses the title of the suppressed see which he formerly had. Other Coadjutors retain this title.[11]

According to Sipos,[12] excommunication or suspension of the residential Bishop has no effect on the office of any Coadjutor. But if one considers the question of an excommunicated residential Bishop, it seems that a distinction must be made between an *excommunicatus toleratus* and the *excommunicatus vitandus.* The former, after a condemnatory or declaratory sentence, is deprived of the fruits of his office, but not of the office itself.[13] The excommunicated Bishop is forbidden to exercise his office,[14] but since the office of the principal Bishop does not cease, neither does that of his Coadjutor. Canon 429, § 5, directs that if the residential Bishop is under excommunication, suspension, or interdict, the Metropolitan—or, if the Metropolitan is under a censure or fails to act, the senior suffragan Bishop—is to report this to the Holy See, which will then provide for the rule of the diocese. Meanwhile there is nothing to prevent any Coadjutor from using faculties already received from the principal Bishop previous to

---

[9] *AAS,* XII (1920), 41; Bouscaren, *The Canon Law Digest,* I, 211; Sipos, *Enchiridion,* n. 51 (7); *Coronata, Institutiones Iuris Canonici,* I, n. 408.

[10] Wernz, *Ius Decretalium,* II, n. 808 (IV).

[11] Bargilliat, *Praelectiones Juris Canonici,* I, n. 785.

[12] *Loc. cit.*

[13] Can. 2266.

[14] Can. 2263.

the excommunication,[15] but he may not receive any additional delegated powers from the excommunicated Bishop.[16]

The case of the *excommunicatus vitandus,* however, is different, for he is deprived even of the office which he held.[17] It follows therefore that, if the residential Bishop is declared a *vitandus,* not only is the aforementioned canon 429, § 5, to be observed, but the rules of canon 355 are also to be applied unless the Holy See should direct otherwise. The *Coadiutor cum iure successionis* would become the principal Bishop, while the office of an *Auxiliaris* would ordinarily cease. The *Coadiutor datus Sedi* would continue in office as before.

No provision is made in the common law concerning the status of the various kinds of Coadjutors should the diocese to which they are assigned be divided or suppressed. Presumably they would remain in the original diocese in the event that it is divided. In the case of the suppression of a diocese the Holy See would have to reassign the Coadjutor.

Apart from the cessation of the office of the principal Bishop, the office of a Coadjutor Bishop may end in the same manner as that of the principal Bishop, namely through his death, resignation, deprivation, removal, or transfer. Wernz[18] adds absolute and perpetual incapacity as another cause. The death of a Coadjutor is to be reported to the Holy See as soon as possible.

Unless a diocese has a Coadjutor with the right of succession or an Apostolic Administrator, the rule of the diocese passes to the Cathedral Chapter or the diocesan consultors when the office of the residential Bishop ceases.[19] Within eight days the members of the Chapter are to elect a Vicar Capitular, or the diocesan consultors a Diocesan Administrator, who will rule the diocese during its vacancy.[20] Woywod (1880-1941),[21] stated that the Coad-

---

[15] Cf. can. 207, § 1.

[16] Cf. can. 2264.

[17] Can. 2266.

[18] *Ius Decretalium,* II, n. 810 (IV).

[19] Can. 431, § 1.

[20] Can. 432, § 1.

[21] *A Practical Commentary on the Code of Canon Law* (7 ed., 2 vols., edited by Callistus Smith, New York: Joseph F. Wagner, 1943), I, 155.

jutor Bishop has no right to convoke the members of the Chapter or the consultors for this election unless he is himself a member of the Chapter or a consultor.

It is the opinion of Sipos[22] that, when there is a Coadjutor in the diocese, he should be chosen to act as Vicar Capitular during the interregnum. It cannot be established from the common law that the electors must choose the former *Auxiliaris* or the *Coadiutor datus Sedi,* but in view of his episcopal dignity and his intimate knowledge of diocesan affairs, it seems most fitting that he should be selected to rule the diocese during its vacancy. It seems also to have been the opinion of the legislators at the II Plenary Council of Baltimore (1866) that the Coadjutor should have charge of the diocese during its vacancy. This is implied in its ruling that Bishops in the United States who hold Church property in their own name should provide in their last will and testament that the Coadjutor, if they have one, be the heir to this property.[23] This law is no longer effective in the United States since the civil law nowhere requires that the residential Bishop hold property in his own name.

---

[22] Enchiridion, n. 51 (7c).

[23] *Concilii Plenarii Baltimorensis II Acta et Decreta,* n. 189.—*Acta et Decreta Sacrorum Conciliorum Recentiorum, Collectio Lacensis* (7 vols., Friburgi Brisgoviae: Herder, 1870-1890), III, 451.

CONCLUSIONS

1. A direct connection between the office of the *Chorepiscopus* of ancient times and the present office of Coadjutor and Auxiliary Bishops cannot be clearly established, though in many respects they are very similar.

2. Claims of certain medieval authors that the appointment of Coadjutor Bishops was reserved to the Holy See previous to the time of Pope Boniface VIII are only *post-factum* arguments.

3. The office of Coadjutor Bishop with the right of future succession is a comparatively late development, appearing for the first time only shortly before the Council of Trent.

4. The terminology of the Code in reference to Coadjutor Bishops differs in many instances from that of pre-Code legislation. The term *Coadiutor datus Sedi* and the meaning now attached to *Auxiliaris* are new in the Code.

5. The office of episcopal Coadjutorship is an ecclesiastical office in the strict sense.

6. If the principal Bishop has died or is dying, the *Auxiliaris* may not proceed to the canonical possession of his office unless his letter of appointment states that his office is to continue *sede vacante*. Other Coadjutors may in such circumstances take possession of their office.

7. Paragraphs 3 and 4 of canon 351 refer to the *Coadiutor datus Sedi* as well as to the *Coadiutor datus personae*.

8. Ordinarily the Coadjutor Bishop should be appointed as the Vicar General in preference to any other priest of the diocese.

9. The words *"Episcopo prorsus inhabili"* of canon 351, § 2, refer only to a residential Bishop who was incapacitated before the appointment of the Coadjutor by the Holy See. In paragraph 4 of the same canon the word *"functiones"* is to be understood in the general sense of "obligations."

10. Excommunication of the principal Bishop does not cause the cessation of the office of a *Coadiutor datus personae* unless the principal Bishop has been declared a *vitandus*.

BIBLIOGRAPHY

Sources

Acta Apostolicae Sedis, Commentarium Officiale, Romae, 1909-

Acta et Decreta Concilii Plenarii Baltimorensis Tertii, A.D. MDCCCLXXXIV, Baltimorae: Typis Ioannis Murphy Sociorum, 1886.

Acta et Decreta Sacrorum Conciliorum Recentiorum, Collectio Lacensis, 7 vols., Friburgi Brisgoviae, 1870-1890.

Bouscaren, T. Lincoln, *The Canon Law Digest,* 2 vols., Milwaukee: Bruce Publishing Company. Vol. I, 1934. Vol. II, 1943.

Bullarum Diplomatum et Privilegiorum Sanctorum Romanorum Pontificum Taurinensis Editio, 24 vols., Neapoli, 1857-1872.

Canones Apostolorum et Conciliorum Saec. IV-VII, ed. Bruns, 2 vols., Berolini, 1839.

Codex Iuris Canonici Pii X Pontificis Maximi iussu digestus, Benedicti Papae XV auctoritate promulgatus, Romae: Typis Polyglottis Vaticanis, 1917. Reimpressio, 1933.

Codicis Iuris Canonici Fontes cura Emi Petri Card. Gasparri editi, 9 vols., Romae (postea Civitate Vaticana): Typis Polyglottis Vaticanis, 1923-1939 (Vols. VII-IX ed. cura et studio Emi Iustiniani Card. Serédi).

Concilii Tridentini, Diariorum, Actorum, Epistularum, Tractatuum, Nova Collectio. Edidit Societas Goerresiana, 13 vols., Friburgi Brisgoviae: apud B. Herder, 1901-1938.

Corpus Iuris Civilis, edd. Kreuger-Mommsen-Schoell-Kroll, 3 vols., Berolini, 1928-1929.

Corpus Iuris Canonici, ed. Lipsiensis 2. post Aemilii Ludovici Richteri curas . . . instruxit Aemilius Friedberg, Lipsiae: Ex Officina Bernhardi Tauchnitz, 1879-1881. Editio anastatice repetita, Lipsiae: Tauchnitz, 1928.

Decreta Authentica Congregationis Sacrorum Rituum, 6 vols., Romae: ex Typographia Polyglotta, 1898-1927.

Decretales D. Gregorii IX, una cum Glossis Restitutae, Romae, 1582.

Decretum Gratiani emendatum et notationibus illustratum una cum Glossis, Gregorii XIII Pont. Max. iussu editum, 2 vols., Romae, 1582.

Jaffé, Philippus, *Regesta Pontificum Romanorum ab condita Ecclesia ad annum post Christum natum MCXCVIII,* ed. 2. correctam et auctam auspiciis Gulielmi Wattenbach curaverunt S. Loewenfeld, F. Kaltenbrunner, P. Ewald, 2 vols. in 1, Lipsiae: 1885-1888.

Liber Sextus Decretalium D. Bonifacii Papae VIII suae integritati una cum Clementinis et Extravagantibus earumque Glossis restitutis, Romae, 1582.

Mansi, Ioannes Dominicus, *Sacrorum Conciliorum Nova et Amplissima Collectio,* 53 vols. in 60, Parisiis, 1901-1927.

Migne, Jacques Paul, *Patrologiae Cursus Completus, Series Graeca,* 161 vols., Parisiis, 1856-1866.

———, *Patrologiae Cursus Completus, Series Latina,* 221 vols., Parisiis, 1844-1864.

Monumenta Germaniae Historica, Epistolae Selectae, Tomus I, Bonifatii et Lulli Epistolae, ed. Michael Tangl, Berolini: apud Weidmannos, 1916.

Monumenta Germaniae Historica, Epistolae Tomus III, Merowingici et Karolini Aevi I, ed. Ericus Caspar, Berolini: apud Weidmannos, 1925.

Monumenta Germaniae Historica, Epistolae Karolini Aevi IV, Tomus VI, edidit Ernestus Perels, Berolini: apud Weidmannos, 1925.

Monumenta Germaniae Historica, Legum Sectio II, Capitularia Regum Francorum, Tomus II, Pars Prior, edd. Alfredus Boretius et Victor Krause, Hannoverae, 1890.

Monumenta Germaniae Historica, Legum Sectio III, Concilia Aevi Merowingici, Tomus II, Pars II, ed. Albertus Werminghoff, Hannoverae et Lipsiae, 1908.

Monumenta Germaniae Historica, (Vita Bonifatii, auctore Willibaldo), Scriptores Rerum Germanarum, Vitae Sancti Bonifatii, recognovit Wilhelmus Levison, Hannoverae et Lipsiae, 1905.

Monumenta Germaniae Historica, Scriptores, Tomus XIII, ed. G. Waitz, Hannoverae, 1881.

Potthast, Augustus, *Regesta Pontificum Romanorum inde ab anno post Christum natum MCXCVIII ad annum MCCCIV,* 2 vols., Berolini, 1874-1875.

Reference Works

Augustine, Charles, *A Commentary on the New Code of Canon Law,* 8 vols., St. Louis: B. Herder Book Co., 1925-1938. Vol. II, 6 ed., 1936.

Ayrinhac, H. A., *The Constitution of the Church in the New Code of Canon Law,* New York: Blase Benziger, 1925.

Bargilliat, M., *Praelectiones Juris Canonici ad canones novi Codicis redacti,* 37 ed., 2 vols., Parisiis: apud Baston, Berche, et Pagis, 1923.

Benedictus XIV (Prosper Lambertini), *De Synodo Dioecesana,* 2 vols., Romae, 1806.

Beste, U., *Introductio in Codicem,* 2 ed., Collegeville, Minnesota: St. John's Abbey Press, 1944.

Blat, Albertus, *Commentarium Textus Codicis Iuris Canonici,* 6 vols., Romae: Libreria del Collegio Angelico, 1919-1927.

Boich, Henricus, *In Quinque Decretalium Libros Commentaria,* Venetiis, 1576.

Bouix, Dominique, *Tractatus de Episcopo,* 2 vols., Parisiis, 1859.

Cappello, F., *Tractatus Canonico-Moralis de Sacramentis iuxta Codicem Iuris Canonici,* 3 vols. in 6, Taurinorum Angustae: Marietti, 1921-1939. Vol. I, 1921.

Chelodi, Ioannes, *Ius de Personis iuxta Codicem Iuris Canonici, praemisso tractatu de principiis et fontibus I.C.,* 2 ed., a Sac. Ernesto Bartagnolli Tridenti: Libr. Edit. Tridentum, 1927.

Claeys Bouuaert-Simenon, G., *Manuale Juris Canonici,* 3 vols., Gandae et Leodii: apud Auctores, 1930-1931. Vol. I, 3 ed., 1930.

Coronata, Matthaeus Conte a, *Institutiones Iuris Canonici ad usus utriusque cleri et scholarum,* 5 vols., Taurini: Marietti, 1928-1936. Vol. I, 1928.

De Meester, A., *Juris Canonici et Juris Canonico-Civilis Compendium,* nova ed., 3 vols. in 4, Brugis: Desclée, 1921-1928.

Donnelly, Francis B., *The Diocesan Synod,* The Catholic University of America Canon Law Studies, n. 74, Washington, D. C., The Catholic University of America, 1932.

Donnellan, Thomas A., *The Obligation of the Missa pro Populo,* The Catholic University of America Canon Law Studies, n. 155, Washington, D. C.: The Catholic University of America Press, 1942.

Eichmann, E., *Lehrbuch des Kirchenrechts auf Grund des Codex Iuris Canonici,* 2 ed., Paderborn: Ferdinand Schoeningh, 1926.

Fagnanus, Prosper, *Commentaria in Quinque Libros Decretalium,* 4 vols., Venetiis, 1696.

Ferraris, Lucius, *Prompta Bibliotheca, Canonica, Juridica, Moralis, Theologica, necnon Ascetica, Polemica, Rubricistica, Historica,* 8 vols., Petit-Montrouge, 1852.

Garcias, Nicolaus, *Tractatus de Beneficiis,* Venetiis, 1618.

Gottlob, Theodor, *Der abendländische Chorepiskopat,* Bonn: Kurt Schroeder, 1928.

Hinschius, Paulus, *Decretales Pseudo-Isidorianae et Capitula Angilramni,* Lipsiae, 1863.

———, *System des katholischen Kirchenrechts,* 4 vols., Berlin, 1869-1888.

Hostiensis, Cardinalis (Henricus de Segusio), *In Quinque Decretalium Libros Commentaria,* 5 vols. in 3, Venetiis, 1581.

Ioannes Andreae, *Commentaria in Quinque Decretalium Libros Novella,* Venetiis, 1581.

Kurtscheid, Bertrand, *Historia Iuris Canonici,* Romae: Officium Libri Catholici, 1941.

McDevitt, Gerald V., *The Renunciation of An Ecclesiastical Office,* The Catholic University of America Canon Law Studies, n. 218, Washington, D. C.: The Catholic University of America Press, 1946.

Navarrus (Martinus de Azpilcueta), *Omnia Opera,* 6 vols., Venetiis, 1618-1621. (Vol. V. *Consiliorum in Quinque Libros et Titulos Decretalium Tomi Duo.*)

O'Neill, William H., *Papal Rescripts of Favor,* The Catholic University of America Canon Law Studies, n. 57, Washington, D. C.: The Catholic University of America, 1930.

Panormitanus, Abbas (Nicolaus de Tudeschis), *Commentaria in Quinque Decretalium Libros,* 5 vols. in 7, Venetiis, 1588.

Piasecius, Paulus, *Praxis Episcopalis, ea quae officium et potestatem Episcopi concernunt continens,* Coloniae Agrippinae, 1620.

Pirhing, Enricus, *Ius Canonicum, Nova Methodo Explicatum,* 5 vols. in 4, Dilingae, 1674-1678.

Prince, John E., *The Diocesan Chancellor,* The Catholic University of America Canon Law Studies, n. 167, Washington, D. C.: The Catholic University of America Press, 1942.

Raus, J. B., *Institutiones Canonicae juxta novum codicem juris pro scholis vel ad usum privatum synthetice redactae,* 2 ed., Lugduni et Parisiis: Typis Emmanuelis Vitte, 1931.

Reiffenstuel, Anacletus, *Jus Canonicum Universum,* 5 vols. in 7, Parisiis, 1864-1870.

Rufinus, *Summa Decretorum,* ed. Heinrich Singer, Paderborn, 1902.

Schmalzgrueber, *Jus Ecclesiasticum Universum,* 5 vols. in 12, Romae, 1843-1845.

Sebastianelli, *Praelectiones Juris Canonici, De Personis,* 2 ed., Romae: Fredericus Pustet, 1905.

Sipos, Stephanus, *Enchiridion Iuris Canonici ad usum scholarum et privatorum,* Pécs: ex Typographia "Haladás R. J.," 1926.

Smith, S. B., *Elements of Ecclesiastical Law, adapted especially to the discipline of the Church in the United States,* 9 ed., 3 vols., New York: Benziger Bros., 1887-1888. Vol. I, *Ecclesiastical Persons,* 1887.

Thomassinus, Ludovicus, *Vetus et Nova Ecclesiae Disciplina circa Beneficia et Beneficiarios,* 10 vols. in 5, Magontiaci, 1787.

Toso, A., *Ad Codicem Iuris Canonici Commentaria Minora,* 5 vols., Romae: Marietti, 1920-1927. Vol. III, 1923.

Vermeersch, A.—Creusen, I., *Epitome Iuris Canonici,* 2 ed., 3 vols., Mechlinae-Romae: H. Dessain, 1924.

Wernz, F. X., *Ius Decretalium,* 6 vols., Romae et Prati: ex Typographia Polyglotta, 1898-1905. Vol. II, *Ius Constitutionis Ecclesiae Catholicae,* 1899.

Wernz, F. X.-Vidal P., *Ius Canonicum ad Codicis normam exactum,* 7 vols. in 8, Romae: apud Aedes Universitatis Gregorianae, 1923-1938.

Woywod, S., *A Pactical Commentary on the Code of Canon Law,* 7 ed., edited by Callistus Smith, 2 vols., New York: Joseph F. Wagner, 1943.

Periodical

Jurist, The, Washington, D. C.: The Catholic University of America, 1941-

Article

Bastnagel, C., "The *Vicarius Adiutor* and the *Missa pro populo,*" *The Jurist,* V (1945), 125-128.

ABBREVIATIONS

AAS—*Acta Apostolicae Sedis.*
Conc. Trident.—*Concilium Tridentinum.*
D.—Digestum (Iustinianum).
Decr. Auth.—*Decreta Authentica.*
Fontes—*Codicis Iuris Canonici Fontes . . . cura . . . Gasparri editi.*
Jaffé—*Regesta Pontificum Romanorum, etc.*
Mansi—*Sacrorum Conciliorum Nova et Amplissima Collectio.*
MGH—*Monumenta Germaniae Historica.*
MPG—Migne, *Patrologia Graeca.*
MPL—Migne, *Patrologia Latina.*
Potthast—*Regesta Pontificum Romanorum, etc.*
S.C.Consist.—Sacra Congregatio Consistorialis.
S.C.Ep. et Reg.—Sacra Congregatio Episcoporum et Regularium.
S.R.C.—Sacrorum Rituum Congregatio.

BIOGRAPHICAL NOTE

George Edward Lynch was born on March 4, 1917, in New York City. He attended St. Barnabas' Parochial School and Regis High School of that city. In September of 1934 he enrolled at Fordham University, receiving the Bachelor of Arts degree in 1938. In the same year he was accepted as a candidate for the priesthood by the Diocese of Raleigh, North Carolina. After a year of Philosophy at Mount St. Mary's Seminary at Emmitsburg, Maryland, he entered the Theological College of the Catholic University of America in September of 1939, and received the degree of S.T.L. in May of 1943. On May 29, 1943, he was ordained to the Holy Priesthood in Washington, D. C. In the fall of that year he enrolled in the School of Canon Law of the Catholic University of America, and received the degree of J.C.B. in May of 1944, and the degree of J.C.L. in May of 1945.

ALPHABETICAL INDEX

CANON LAW STUDIES*

1. Freriks, Rev. Celestine A., C.PP.S., J.C.D., Religious Congregations in Their External Relations, 121 pp., 1916.
2. Galliher, Rev. Daniel M., O.P., J.C.D., Canonical Elections, 117 pp., 1917.
3. Borkowski, Rev. Aurelius L., O.F.M., J.C.D., De Confraternitatibus Ecclesiasticis, 136 pp., 1918.
4. Castillo, Rev. Cayo, J.C.D., Disertacion Historico-Canonica sobre la Potestad del Cabildo en Sede Vacante o Impedida del Vicario Capitular, 99 pp., 1919 (1918).
5. Kubelbeck, Rev. William J., S.T.B., J.C.D., The Sacred Penitentiaria and Its Relation to Faculties of Ordinaries and Priests, 129 pp., 1918.
6. Petrovits, Rev. Joseph J. C., S.T.D., J.C.D., The New Church Law on Matrimony, X-461 pp., 1919.
7. Hickey, Rev. John J., S.T.B., J.C.D., Irregularities and Simple Impediments in the New Code of Canon Law, 100 pp., 1920.
8. Klekotka, Rev. Peter J., S.T.B., J.C.D., Diocesan Consultors, 179 pp., 1920.
9. Wanenmacher, Rev. Francis, J.C.D., The Evidence in Ecclesiastical Procedure Affecting the Marriage Bond, 1920 (Printed 1935).
10. Golden, Rev. Henry Francis, J.C.D., Parochial Benefices in the New Code, IV-119 pp., 1921 (Printed 1925).
11. Koudelka, Rev. Charles J., J.C.D., Pastors, Their Rights and Duties According to the New Code of Canon Law, 211 pp., 1921.
12. Melo, Rev. Antonius, O.F.M., J.C.D., De Exemptione Regularium, X-188 pp., 1921.
13. Schaaf, Rev. Valentine Theodore, O.F.M., S.T.B., J.C.D., The Cloister, X-180 pp., 1921.
14. Burke, Rev. Thomas Joseph, S.T.D., J.C.D., Competence in Ecclesiastical Tribunals, IV-117 pp., 1922.
15. Leech, Rev. George Leo, J.C.D., A Comparative Study of the Constitution "Apostolicae Sedis" and the "Codex Juris Canonici," 179 pp., 1922.
16. Motry, Rev. Hubert Louis, S.T.D., J.C.D., Diocesan Faculties According to the Code of Canon Law, II-167 pp., 1922.
17. Murphy, Rev. George Lawrence, J.C.D., Delinquencies and Penalties in the Administration and the Reception of the Sacraments, IV-121 pp., 1923.

* Below n. 100 only the following numbers are still available: Nn. 3, 4, 9, 25, 34, 57 and 75. Beginning with n. 100 only the following are unavailable: Nn. 100-111 inclusive, and n. 113.

18. O'Reilly, Rev. John Anthony, S.T.B., J.C.D., Ecclesiastical Sepulture in the New Code of Canon Law, 11-129 pp., 1923.
19. Michalicka, Rev. Wenceslas Cyril, O.S.B., J.C.D., Judicial Procedure in Dismissal of Clerical Exempt Religious, 107 pp., 1923.
20. Dargin, Rev. Edward Vincent, S.T.B., J.C.D., Reserved Cases According to the Code of Canon Law, IV-103 pp., 1924.
21. Godfrey, Rev. John A., S.T.B., J.C.D., The Right of Patronage According to the Code of Canon Law, 153 pp., 1924.
22. Hagedorn, Rev. Francis Edward, J.C.D., General Legislation on Indulgences, II-154 pp., 1924.
23. King, Rev. James Ignatius, J.C.D., The Administration of the Sacraments to Dying Non-Catholics, V-141 pp., 1924.
24. Winslow, Rev. Francis Joseph, O.F.M., J.C.D., Vicars and Prefects Apostolic, IV-149 pp., 1924.
25. Correa, Rev. Jose Servelion, S.T.L., J.C.D., La Potestad Legislativa de la Iglesia Catolica, IV-127 pp., 1925.
26. Dugan, Rev. Henry Francis, A.M., J.C.D., The Judiciary Department of the Diocesan Curia, 87 pp., 1925.
27. Keller, Rev. Charles Frederick, S.T.B., J.C.D., Mass Stipends, 167 pp., 1925.
28. Paschang, Rev. John Linus, J.C.D., The Sacramentals According to the Code of Canon Law, 129 pp., 1925.
29. Piontek, Rev. Cyrillus, O.F.M., S.T.B., J.C.D., De Indulto Exclaustrationis necnon Saecularizationis, XIII-289 pp., 1925.
30. Kearney, Rev. Richard Joseph, S.T.B., J.C.D., Sponsors at Baptism According to the Code of Canon Law, IV-127 pp., 1925.
31. Bartlett, Rev. Chester Joseph, A.M., LL.B., J.C.D., The Tenure of Parochial Property in the United States of America, V-108 pp., 1926.
32. Kilker, Rev. Adrian Jerome, J.C.D., Extreme Unction, V-425 pp., 1926.
33. McCormick, Rev. Robert Emmett, J.C.D., Confessors of Religious, VIII-266 pp., 1926.
34. Miller, Rev. Newton Thomas, J.C.D., Founded Masses According to the Code of Canon Law, VII-93 pp., 1926.
35. Roelker, Rev. Edward G., S.T.D., J.C.D., Principles of Privilege According to the Code of Canon Law, XI-166 pp., 1926.
36. Bakalarczyk, Rev. Richardus, M.I.C., J.U.D., De Novitiatu, VIII-208 pp., 1927.
37. Pizzuti, Rev. Lawrence, O.F.M., J.U.L., De Parochis Religiosis, 1927. (Not Printed.)
38. Bliley, Rev. Nicholas Martin, O.S.B., J.C.D., Altars According to the Code of Canon Law, XIX-132 pp., 1927.
39. Brown, Mr. Brendan Francis, A.B., LL.M., J.U.D., The Canonical Juristic Personality with Special Reference to its Status in the United States of America, V-212 pp., 1927.

40. Cavanaugh, Rev. William Thomas, C.P., J.U.D., The Reservation of the Blessed Sacrament, VIII-101 pp., 1927.
41. Doheny, Rev. William J., C.S.C., A.B., J.U.D., Church Property: Modes of Acquisition, X-118 pp., 1927.
42. Feldhaus, Rev. Aloysius H., C.PP.S., J.C.D., Oratories, IX-141 pp., 1927.
43. Kelly, Rev. James Patrick, A.B., J.C.D., The Jurisdiction of the Simple Confessor, X-208 pp., 1927.
44. Neuberger, Rev. Nicholas J., J.C.D., Canon 6 or the Relation of the Codex Juris Canonici to the Preceding Legislation, V-95 pp., 1927.
45. O'Keefe, Rev. Gerald Michael, J.C.D., Matrimonial Dispensations, Powers of Bishops, Priests, and Confessors, VIII-232 pp., 1927.
46. Quigley, Rev. Joseph A. M., A.B., J.C.D., Condemned Societies, 139 pp., 1927.
47. Zaplotnik, Rev. Johannes Leo, J.C.D., De Vicariis Foraneis, X-142 pp., 1927.
48. Duskie, Rev. John Aloysius, A.B., J.C.D., The Canonical Status of the Orientals in the United States, VIII-196 pp., 1928.
49. Hyland, Rev. Francis Edward, J.C.D., Excommunication, Its Nature, Historical Development and Effects, VIII-181 pp., 1928.
50. Reinmann, Rev. Gerald Joseph, O.M.C., J.C.D., The Third Order Secular of Saint Francis, 201 pp., 1928.
51. Schenk, Rev. Francis J., J.C.D., The Matrimonial Impediments of Mixed Religion and Disparity of Cult, XVI-318 pp., 1929.
52. Coady, Rev. John Joseph, S.T.D., J.U.D., A.M., The Appointment of Pastors, VIII-150 pp., 1929.
53. Kay, Rev. Thomas Henry, J.C.D., Competence in Matrimonial Procedure, VIII-164 pp., 1929.
54. Turner, Rev. Sidney Joseph, C.P., J.U.D., The Vow of Poverty, XLIX-217 pp., 1929.
55. Kearney, Rev. Raymond A., A.B., S.T.D., J.C.D., The Principles of Delegation, VII-149 pp., 1929.
56. Conran, Rev. Edward James, A.B., J.C.D., The Interdict, V-163 pp., 1930.
57. O'Neill, Rev. William H., J.C.D., Papal Rescripts of Favor, VII-218 pp., 1930.
58. Bastnagel, Rev. Clement Vincent, J.U.D., The Appointment of Parochial Adjutants and Assistants, XV-257 pp., 1930.
59. Ferry, Rev. William A., A.B., J.C.D., Stole Fees, V-136 pp., 1930.
60. Costello, Rev. John Michael, A.B., J.C.D., Domicile and Quasi-Domicile, VII-201 pp., 1930.
61. Kremer, Rev. Michael Nicholas, A.B., S.T.B., J.C.D., Church Support in the United States, VI-136 pp., 1930.
62. Angulo, Rev. Luis, C.M., J.C.D., Legislation de la Iglesia sobre la intencion en la application de la Santa Misa, VII-104 pp., 1931.

63. Frey, Rev. Wolfgang Norbert, O.S.B., A.B., J.C.D., The Act of Religious Profession, VIII-174 pp., 1931.
64. Roberts, Rev. James Brendan, A.B., J.C.D., The Banns of Marriage, XIV-140 pp., 1931.
65. Ryder, Rev. Raymond Aloysius, A.B., J.C.D., Simony, IX-151 pp., 1931.
66. Campagna, Rev. Angelo, Ph.D., J.U.D., Il Vicario Generale del Vescovo, VII-205 pp., 1931.
67. Cox, Rev. Joseph Godfrey, A.B., J.C.D., The Administration of Seminaries, VI-124 pp., 1931.
68. Gregory, Rev. Donald J., J.U.D., The Pauline Privilege, XV-165 pp., 1931.
69. Donohue, Rev. John F., J.C.D., The Impediment of Crime, VII-110 pp., 1931.
70. Dooley, Rev. Eugene A., O.M.I., J.C.D., Church Law on Sacred Relics, IX-143 pp., 1931.
71. Orth, Rev. Clement Raymond, O.M.C., J.C.D., The Approbation of Religious Institutes, 171 pp., 1931.
72. Pernicone, Rev. Joseph M., A.B., J.C.D., The Ecclesiastical Prohibition of Books, XII-267 pp., 1932.
73. Clinton, Rev. Connell, A.B., J.C.D., The Paschal Precept, IX-108 pp., 1932.
74. Donnelly, Rev. Francis B,. A.M., S.T.L., J.C.D., The Diocesan Synod, VIII-125 pp., 1932.
75. Torrente, Rev. Camilo, C.M.F., J.C.D., Las Procesiones Sagradas, V-145 pp., 1932.
76. Murphy, Rev. Edwin J., C.PP.S., J.C.D., Suspension Ex Informata Conscientia, XI-122 pp., 1932.
77. MacKenzie, Rev. Eric F., A.M., S.T.L., J.C.D., The Delict of Heresy in its Commission, Penalization, Absolution, VII-124 pp., 1932.
78. Lyons, Rev. Avitus E., S.T.B., J.C.D., The Collegiate Tribunal of First Instance, XI-147 pp., 1932.
79. Connolly, Rev. Thomas A., J.C.D., Appeals, XI-195 pp., 1932.
80. Sangmeister, Rev. Joseph V., A.B., J.C.D., Force and Fear as Precluding Matrimonial Consent, V-211 pp., 1932.
81. Jaeger, Rev. Leo A., A.B., J.C.D., The Administration of Vacant and Quasi-Vacant Episcopal Sees in the United States, IX-229 pp., 1932.
82. Rimlinger, Rev. Herbert T., J.C.D., Error Invalidating Matrimonial Consent, VII-79 pp., 1932.
83. Barrett, Rev. John D. M., S.S., J.C.D., A Comparative Study of the Third Plenary Council of Baltimore and the Code, IX-221 pp., 1932.
84. Carberry, Rev. John J., Ph.D., S.T.D., J.C.D., The Juridical Form of Marriage, X-177 pp., 1934.
85. Dolan, Rev. John L., A.B., J.C.D., The Defensor Vinculi, XII-157 pp., 1934.

86. HANNAN, REV. JEROME D., A.M., S.T.D., LL.B., J.C.D., The Canon Law of Wills, IX-517 pp., 1934.
87. LEMIEUX, REV. DELISE A., A.M., J.C.D., The Sentence in Ecclesiastical Procedure, IX-131 pp., 1934.
88. O'ROURKE, REV. JAMES J., A.B., J.C.D., Parish Registers, VII-109 pp., 1934.
89. TIMLIN, REV. BARTHOLOMEW, O.F.M., A.M., J.C.D., Conditional Matrimonial Consent, X-381 pp., 1934.
90. WAHL, REV. FRANCIS X., A.B., J.C.D., The Matrimonial Impediments of Consanguinity and Affinity, VI-125 pp., 1934.
91. WHITE, REV. ROBERT J., A.B., LL.B., S.T.B., J.C.D., Canonical Ante-Nuptial Promises and the Civil Law, VI-152 pp., 1934.
92. HERRERA, REV. ANTONIO PARRA, O.C.D., J.C.D., Legislacion Ecclesiastica sobra el Ayuno y la Abstinencia, XI-191 pp., 1935.
93. KENNEDY, REV. EDWIN J., J.C.D., The Special Matrimonial Process in Cases of Evident Nullity, X-165 pp., 1935.
94. MANNING, REV. JOHN J., A.B., J.C.D., Presumption of Law in Matrimonial Procedure, XI-111 pp., 1935.
95. MOEDER, REV. JOHN M., J.C.D., The Proper Bishop for Ordination and Dimissorial Letters, VII-135 pp., 1935.
96. O'MARA, REV. WILLIAM A., A.B., J.C.D., Canonical Causes for Matrimonial Dispensations, IX-155 pp., 1935.
97. REILLY, REV. PETER, J.C.D., Residence of Pastors, IX-81 pp., 1935.
98. SMITH, REV. MARINER T., O.P., S.T.Lr., J.C.D., The Penal Law for Religious, VII-169 pp., 1935.
99. WHALEN, REV. DONALD W., A.M., J.C.D., The Value of Testimonial Evidence in Matrimonial Procedure, XIII-297 pp., 1935.
100. CLEARY, REV. JOSEPH F., J.C.D., Canonical Limitations on the Alienation of Church Property, VIII-141 pp., 1936.
101. GLYNN, REV. JOHN C., J.C.D., The Promoter of Justice, XX-337 pp., 1936.
102. BRENNAN, REV. JAMES H., S.S., M.A., S.T.B., J.C.D., The Simple Convalidation of Marriage, VI-135 pp., 1937.
103. BBUNINI, REV. JOSEPH BERNARD, J.C.D., The Clerical Obligations of Canons 139 and 142, X-121 pp., 1937.
104. CONNOR, REV. MAURICE, A.B., J.C.D., The Administrative Removal of Pastors, VIII-159 pp., 1937.
105. GUILFOYLE, REV. MERLIN JOSEPH, J.C.D., Custom, XI-144 pp., 1937.
106. HUGHES, REV. JAMES AUSTIN, A.B., A.M., J.C.D., Witnesses in Criminal Trials of Clerics, IX-140 pp., 1937.
107. JANSEN, REV. RAYMOND J., A.B., S.T.L., J.C.D., Canonical Provisions for Catechetical Instruction, VII-153 pp., 1937.
108. KEALY, REV. JOHN JAMES, A.B., J.C.D., The Introductory Libellus in Church Court Procedure, XI-121 pp., 1937.
109. MCMANUS, REV. JAMES EDWARD, C.SS.R., J.C.D., The Administration of Temporal Goods in Religious Institutes, XVI-196 pp., 1937.

110. Moriarty, Rev. Eugene James, J.C.D., Oaths in Ecclesiastical Courts, X-115 pp., 1937.
111. Rainer, Rev. Eligius George, C.SS.R., J.C.D., Suspension of Clerics, XVII-249 pp., 1937.
112. Reilly, Rev. Thomas F., C.SS.R., J.C.D., Visitation of Religious, VI-195 pp., 1938.
113. Moriarity, Rev. Francis E., C.SS.R., J.C.D., The Extraordinary Absolution from Censures, XV-334 pp., 1938.
114. Connolly, Rev. Nicholas P., J.C.D., The Canonical Erection of Parishes, X-132 pp., 1938.
115. Donovan, Rev. James Joseph, J.C.D., The Pastor's Obligation in Prenuptial Investigation, XII-322 pp., 1938.
116. Harrigan, Rev. Robert J., M.A., S.T.B., J.C.D., The Radical Sanation of Invalid Marriages, VIII-208 pp., 1938.
117. Boffa, Rev. Conrad Humbert, J.C.D., Canonical Provisions for Catholic Schools, VII-211 pp., 1939.
118. Parsons, Rev. Anscar John, O.M.Cap., J.C.D., Canonical Elections, XII-236 pp., 1939.
119. Reilly, Rev. Edward Michael, A.B., J.C.D., The General Norms of Dispensation, XII-156 pp., 1939.
120. Ryan, Rev. Gerald Aloysius, A.B., J.C.D., Principles of Episcopal Jurisdiction, XII-172 pp., 1939.
121. Burton, Rev. Francis James, C.S.C., A.B., J.C.D., A Commentary on Canon 1125, X-222 pp., 1940.
122. Miaskiewicz, Rev. Francis Sigismund, J.C.D., Supplied Jurisdiction According to Canon 209, XII-340 pp., 1940.
123. Rice, Rev. Patrick William, A.B., J.C.D., Proof of Death in Prenuptial Investigation, VIII-156 pp., 1940.
124. Anglin, Rev. Thomas Francis, M.S., J.C.D., The Eucharistic Fast, VIII-183 pp., 1941.
125. Coleman, Rev. John Jerome, J.C.D., The Minister of Confirmation, VI-153 pp., 1941.
126. Downs, Rev. Joseph Emmanuel, A.B., J.C.D., The Concept of Clerical Immunity, XI-163 pp., 1941.
127. Esswein, Rev. Anthony Albert, J.C.D., Extrajudicial Penal Powers of Ecclesiastical Superiors, X-144 pp., 1941.
128. Farrell, Rev. Benjamin Francis, M.A., S.T.L., J.C.D., The Rights and Duties of the Local Ordinary Regarding Congregations of Women Religious of Pontifical Approval, V-195 pp., 1941.
129. Feeney, Rev. Thomas John, A.B., S.T.L., J.C.D., Restitutio in Integrum, VI-169 pp., 1941.
130. Findlay, Rev. Stephen William, O.S.B., A.B., J.C.D., Canonical Norms Governing the Deposition and Degradation of Clerics, XVII-279 pp., 1941.
131. Goodwine, Rev. John, A.B., S.T.L., J.C.D., The Right of the Church to Acquire Property, VIII-119 pp., 1941.

132. Heston, Rev. Edward Louis, C.S.C., Ph.D., S.T.D., J.C.D., The Alienation of Church Property in the United States, XII-222 pp., 1941.
133. Hogan, Rev. James John, A.B., S.T.L., J.C.D., Judicial Advocates and Procurators, XIII-200 pp., 1941.
134. Kealy, Rev. Thomas M., A.B., Litt.D., J.C.D., Dowry of Women Religious, IX-152 pp., 1941.
135. Keene, Rev. Michael James, O.S.B., J.C.D., Religious Ordinaries and Canon 198, V-164 pp., 1942.
136. Kerin, Rev. Charles A., S.S., M.A., S.T.B., J.C.D., The Privation of Christian Burial, XVI-279 pp., 1941.
137. Louis, Rev. William Francis, M.A., J.C.D., Diocesan Archives, X-101 pp., 1941.
138. McDevitt, Rev. Gilbert Joseph, A.B., J.C.D., Legitimacy and Legitimation, X-247 pp., 1941.
139. McDonough, Rev. Thomas Joseph, A.B., J.C.D., Apostolic Administrators, X-217 pp., 1941.
140. Meier, Rev. Carl Anthony, A.B., J.C.D., Penal Administration Procedure Against Negligent Pastors, XI-240 pp., 1941.
141. Schmidt, Rev. John Rogg, A.B., J.C.D., The Principles of Authentic Interpretation in Canon 17 of the Code of Canon Law, XII-331 pp., 1941.
142. Slafkosky, Rev. Andrew Leonard, A.B., J.C.D., The Canonical Episcopal Visitation of the Diocese, X-197 pp., 1941.
143. Swoboda, Rev. Innocent Robert, O.F.M., J.C.D., Ignorance in Relation to the Imputability of Delicts, IX-271 pp., 1941.
144. Dubé, Rev. Arthur Joseph, A.B., J.C.D., The General Principles for the Reckoning of Time in Canon Law, VIII-299 pp., 1941.
145. McBride, Rev. James T., A.B., J.C.D., Incardination and Excardination of Seculars, XX-585 pp., 1941.
146. Krol, Rev. John T., J.C.D., The Defendant in Ecclesiastical Trials, XII-207 pp., 1942.
147. Comyns, Rev. Joseph J., C.SS.R., A.B., J.C.D., Papal and Episcopal Administration of Church Property, XIV-155 pp., 1942.
148. Barry, Rev. Garrett Francis, O.M.I., J.C.D., Violation of the Cloister, XII-260 pp., 1942.
149. Bolduc, Rev. Gatien, C.S.V., A.B., S.T.L., J.C.D., Les Études dans les Religions Cléricales, VIII-155 pp., 1942.
150. Boyle, Rev. David John, M.A., J.C.D., The Juridic Effects of Moral Certitude on Pre-Nuptial Guarantees, XII-188 pp., 1942.
151. Canavan, Rev. Walter Joseph, M.A., Litt.D., J.C.D., The Profession of Faith, XII-143 pp., 1942.
152. Desrochers, Rev. Bruno, A.B., Ph.L., S.T.B., J.C.D., Le Premier Concile Plénier de Québec et le Code de Droit Canonique, XIV-186 pp., 1942.

153. Dillon, Rev. Robert Edward, A.B., J.C.D., Common Law Marriage, X-148 pp., 1942.
154. Dodwell, Rev. Edward John, Ph.D., S.T.B., J.C.D., The Time and Place for the Celebration of Marriage, X-156 pp., 1942.
155. Donnellan, Rev. Thomas Andrew, A.B., J.C.D., The Obligation of the Misa pro Populo, VII-131 pp., 1942.
156. Eltz, Rev. Louis Anthony, A.B., J.C.L., Cooperation in Crime.
157. Gass, Rev. Sylvester Francis, M.A., J.C.D., Ecclesiastical Pensions, XI-206 pp., 1942.
158. Guiniven, Rev. John Joseph, C.SS.R., J.C.D., The Precept of Hearing Mass, XIV-188 pp., 1942.
159. Gulczynski, Rev. John Theophilus, J.C.D., The Desecration and Violation of Churches, X-126 pp., 1942.
160. Hammill, Rev. John Leo, M.A., J.C.D., The Obligations of the Traveler According to Canon 14, VIII-204 pp., 1942.
161. Haydt, Rev. John Joseph, A.B., J.C.D., Reserved Benefices, XI-148 pp., 1942.
162. Huser, Rev. Roger John, O.F.M., A.B., J.C.D., The Crime of Abortion in Canon Law, XII-187 pp., 1942.
163. Kearney, Rev. Francis Patrick, A.B., S.T.L., J.C.L., The Principles of Canon 1127
164. Linahen, Rev. Leo James, S.T.L., J.C.D., De Absolutione Complicis In Peccato Turpi, 114 pp., 1942.
165. McCloskey, Rev. Joseph Aloysius, A.B., J.C.D., The Subject of Ecclesiastical Law According to Canon 12, XVII-246 pp., 1942.
166. O'Neill, Rev. Francis Joseph, C.SS.R., J.C.D., The Dismissal of Religious in Temporary Vows, XIII-220 pp., 1942.
167. Prince, Rev. John Edward, A.B., S.T.D., J.C.D., The Diocesan Chancellor, X-136 pp., 1942.
168. Riesner, Rev. Albert Joseph, C.SS.R., J.C.D., Apostates and Fugitives from Religious Institutes, IX-168 pp., 1942.
169. Stenger, Rev. Joseph Bernard, J.C.D., The Mortgaging of Church Property, 186 pp., 1942.
170. Waldron, Rev. Joseph Francis, A.B., J.C.D., The Minister of Baptism, XII-197 pp., 1942.
171. Willett, Rev. Robert Albert, J.C.D., The Probative Value of Documents in Ecclesiastical Trials, X-124 pp., 1942.
172. Woeber, Rev. Edward Martin, M.A., J.C.D., The Interpellations, XII-161 pp., 1942.
173. Benko, Rev. Matthew Aloysius, O.S.B., M.A., J.C.L., The Abbot *Nullius*.
174. Christ, Rev. Joseph James, M.A., S.T.L., J.C.L., Dispensation from Vindicative Penalties.
175. Clancy, Rev. Patrick M. J., O.P., A.B., S.T.Lr., J.C.D., The Local Religious Superior, X-299 pp., 1943.

176. Clarke, Rev. Thomas James, J.C.D., Parish Societies, XII-147 pp.. 1943.
177. Connolly, Rev. John Patrick, S.T.L., J.C.D., Synodal Examiners and Parish Priest Consultors, X-223 pp., 1943.
178. Drumm, Rev. William Martin, A.B., J.C.L., Hospital Chaplains.
179. Flanagan, Rev. Bernard Joseph, A.B., S.T.L., J.C.D., The Canonical Erection of Religious Houses, X-147 pp., 1943.
180. Kelleher, Rev. Stephen Joseph, A.B., S.T.B., J.C.D., Discussions with non-Catholics: Canonical Legislation, X-93 pp., 1943.
181. Lewis, Rev. Gordian, C.P., J.C.D., Chapters in Religious Institutes, XII-169 pp., 1943.
182. Marx, Rev. Adolph, J.C.D., The Declaration of Nullity of Marriages Contracted Outside the Church, X-151 pp., 1943.
183. Matulenas, Rev. Raymond Anthony, O.S.B., A.B., J.C.L., Communication, a Source of Privileges.
184. O'Leary, Rev. Charles Gerard, C.SS.R., J.C.D., Religious Dismissed After Perpetual Profession, X-213 pp., 1943.
185. Power, Rev. Cornelius Michael, J.C.L., The Blessing of Cemeteries.
186. Shuhler, Rev. Ralph Vincent, O.S.A., J.C.D., Privileges of Regulars to Absolve and Dispense, XII-195 pp., 1943.
187. Ziolkowski, Rev. Thaddeus Stanislaus, A.B., J.C.D., The Consecration and Blessing of Churches, XII-151 pp., 1943.
188. Heneghan, Rev. John Joseph, S.T.D., J.C.L., The Marriages of Unworthy Catholics: Canons 1065 and 1066.
189. Carroll, Rev. Coleman Francis, M.A., S.T.L., J.C.L., Charitable Institutions.
190. Ciesluk, Rev. Joseph Edward, Ph.B., S.T.L., J.C.L., National Parishes in the United States.
191. Coburn, Rev. Vincent Paul, A.B., J.C.L., Marriages of Conscience.
192. Connors, Rev. Charles Paul, C.S.Sp., A.B., J.C.L., Extra-Judicial Procurators in the Code of Canon Law.
193. Coyle, Rev. Paul Raymond, A.B., J.C.L., Judicial Exceptions.
194. Fair, Rev. Bartholomew Francis, A.B., S.T.L., J.C.L., The Impediment of Abduction.
195. Gallagher, Rev. Thomas Raphael, O.P., A.B., S.T.Lr., J.C.L., The Examination of the Qualities of the Ordinand.
196. Gannon, Rev. John Mark, S.T.L., J.C.L., The Interstices Required for the Promotion to Orders.
197. Goldsmith, Rev. J. William, B.C.S., S.T.L., J.C.L., The Competence of Church and State over Marriage—Disputed Points.
198. Goodwine, Rev. Joseph Gerard, A.B., S.T.B., J.C.L., The Reception of Converts.
199. Kowalski, Rev. Romuald Eugene, O.F.M., A.B., J.C.L., Sustenance of Religious Houses of Regulars.
200. McCoy, Rev. Alan Edward, O.F.M., J.C.L., Force and Fear in Relation to Delictual Imputability and Penal Responsibility.

201. McDevitt, Rev. Vincent John, Ph.B., S.T.L., J.C.L., Perjury.
202. Martin, Rev. Thomas Owen, Ph.D., S.T.D., J.C.L., Adverse Possession, Prescription and Limitation of Actions: The Canonical "Praescriptio."
203. Miklosovic, Rev. Paul John, A.B., J.C.L., Attempted Marriages and Their Consequent Juridic Effects.
204. Mundy, Rev. Thomas Maurice, A.B., S.T.L., J.C.L., The Union of Parishes.
205. O'Dea, Rev. John Coyle, A.B., J.C.L., The Matrimonial Impediment of Nonage.
206. Olalia, Rev. Alexander Ayson, S.T.L., J.C.L., A Comparative Study of the Christian Constitution of States and the Constitution of the Philippine Commonwealth.
207. Poisson, Rev. Pierre-Marie, C.S.C., A.B., Ph.L., Th.L., J.C.L., Droits Patrimoniaux des Maisons et des Eglises Religieuses.
208. Stadalnikas, Rev. Casimir Joseph, M.I.C., J.C.L., Reservation of Censures.
209. Sullivan, Rev. Eugene Henry, S.T.L., J.C.L., Proof of the Reception of the Sacraments.
210. Vaughan, Rev. William Edward, J.C.L., Constitutions for Diocesan Courts.
211. Paro, Rev. Gino, S.T.D., J.C.L., The Right of Apostolic Legation.
212. Balzer, Rev. Ralph Francis, C.P., J.C.L., The Computation of Time in a Canonical Novitiate.
213. Dougherty, Rev. John Whelan, A.B., S.T.L., J.C.L., De Inquisitione Speciali.
214. Dziob, Rev. Michael Walter, J.C.L., The Sacred Congregation for the Oriental Church.
215. Eidenschink, Rev. John Albert, O.S.B., B.A., J.C.L., The Election of Bishops in the Letters of Pope Gregory the Great.
216. Gill, Rev. Nicholas, C.P., J.C.L., The Spiritual Prefect in Clerical Religious Houses of Study.
217. Hynes, Rev. Harry Gerard, S.T.L., J.C.D., The Privileges of Cardinals, XII-183 pp., 1945.
218. McDevitt, Rev. Gerald Vincent, S.T.L., J.C.D., The Renunciation of an Ecclesiastical Office, XIV—179 pp., 1946.
219. Manning, Rev. Joseph Leroy, J.C.L., The Free Conferral of Offices.
220. Meyer, Rev. Louis G., O.S.B., A.B., S.T.B., J.C.D., Alms-Gathering by Religious, XII—163 pp., 1946.
221. O'Donnell, Rev. Cletus Francis, M.A., J.C.L., The Marriage of Minors.
222. Prunskis, Rev. Joseph, J.C.D., Comparative Law, Ecclesiastical and Civil, in Lithuanian Concordat, X—161 pp., 1945.
223. Sweeney, Rev. Francis Patrick, C.SS.R., J.C.D., The Reduction of Clerics to the Lay State, X—199 pp., 1945.

224. Vogelpohl, Rev. Henry John, J.C.L., The Simple Impediments to Holy Orders.
225. Brockhaus, Rev. Thomas Aquinas, O.S.B., A.B., J.C.L., Religious who Are Known as *Conversi.*
226. Griese, Rev. Orville Nicholas, S.T.D., J.C.L., Marriage and the Procreation of Offspring.
227. Boudreaux, Rev. Warren Louis, J.C.L., The *"ab acatholicis nati"* of Canon 1099, § 2.
228. Bowe, Rev. Thomas Joseph, A.B., J.C.L., Religious Superioresses.
229. Diederichs, Rev. Michael Ferdinand, S.C.J., J.C.L., The Jurisdiction of the Latin Ordinaries over their Oriental Subjects.
230. Dingman, Rev. Maurice John, A.B., S.T.L., J.C.L., The Plaintiff in Contentious Trials.
231. Frison, Rev. Basil, C.M.F., M.Mus., J.C.L., The Retroactivity of Law.
232. Galvin, Rev. William Anthony, M.A., J.C.L., The Administrative Transfer of Pastors.
233. Goracy, Rev. Joseph C., J.C.L., The Diriment Impediment of Major Orders.
234. Hale, Rev. Joseph Francis, M.A., S.T.L., J.C.L., The Pastor of Burial.
235. Henry, Rev. Joseph Arthur, A.B., J.C.L., The Mass and Holy Communion: Inter-Ritual Law.
236. Linenberger, Rev. Herbert, C.PP.S., J.C.L., The False Denunciation of an Innocent Confessor.
237. Lowry, Rev. James Martin, A.B., J.C.L., Dispensation from Private Vows.
238. Lynch, Rev. George Edward, A.B., S.T.L., J.C.L., Coadjutors and Auxiliaries of Bishops.
239. Lynch, Rev. Timothy, M.S.SS.T., J.C.L., Contracts between Bishops and Religious Congregations.
240. McClunn, Rev. Justin David, A.B., S.T.L., J.C.L., Administrative Recourse.
241. McGarvey, Rev. Thomas Joseph, A.B., S.T.L., J.C.L., Bination.
242. McGrath, Rev. James, A.B., J.C.L., The Privilege of the Canon.
243. Marbach, Rev. Joseph Francis, A.B., J.C.L., Marriage Legislation for the Catholics of the Oriental Rites in the United States and Canada.
244. Shimkus, Rev. Bernard Aloysius, A.B., J.C.L., The Determination and Transfer of Rite.
245. Smith, Rev. Vincent Michael, A.B., S.T.L., J.C.L., Ignorance Affecting Matrimonial Consent.
246. Wachtrle, Rev. Paul Anthony, A.B., J.C.L., The Baptism of the Children of Non-Catholics.

www.ingramcontent.com/pod-product-compliance
Lightning Source LLC
LaVergne TN
LVHW050201080826
844660LV00012B/331

* 9 7 8 0 8 1 3 2 2 4 1 8 3 *